If I Could Be More

Written by Kurt Chunn

Edited and Formatted by Brittany Johnson

Cover by Wesley R. Gardner

Jim,

Thanks for your love for the Lord & His Word, & sharing in such a clear fashion the truths of His Word with others. You have been a real blessing in my life. May God richly bless you as you continue to serve Him,

Yours in Him,

Kurt

Text and photos copyright © 2014 Kurt Chunn

All Rights Reserved

This book is dedicated to my wife Debra, whose love for me sustains me.

Thanks to those who helped review this book and helped to sharpen my focus: Jerry and Janet Leslie of the Austin Avenue church of Christ in Brownwood, Texas; Becky Blackmon, author of *"The Begging Place"*; Dr. Jesse Robertson, Dean of Graduate Studies and Outreach and Assistant Professor of Bible at Freed-Hardeman University and minister at the Estes church of Christ; and Dr. Paul Faulkner, former professor at Abilene Christian University. Their thoughts and suggestions were invaluable.

"My overview is that it is one of the most delightful books I have read in quite a while…Kurt is not just a friend, but a treasure to the kingdom: heart and soul. His easy way of introducing us to the harsh realities and tribulations of life is touching."

– Dr. Paul Faulkner

Introduction: If I Could Be More Like Sadie... 5
...I Would Do What I Was Created to Do! 11
...I Wouldn't Bite! 19
...I Would Have No Worries! 26
...I Would Forgive More Easily! 31
...I Would Find My Master's Presence Comforting! 40
...I Would Enjoy People More! 46
...I Would Be More Joyful! 56
...I Would Listen to My Master's Voice! 67
...I Would Be More Persistent in Prayer! 74
...I Would Long for My Master's Return! 83
The Master's Timing... 90

Introduction: If I Could Be More Like Sadie...

"But ask the animals, and they will teach you..." Job 12:7

Zoomorphism. Now *that's* a word! The dictionary defines it as "the ascriptions of animal form or attributes to beings or things not animal"[1]. Basically, it means attributing animal traits to people (since people are *not just* animals!).

What does this have to do with spiritual development? Well, God in His Word often used "zoomorphism" to teach people how best to live. Consider how God inspired Solomon to use the examples of nature to teach important life lessons. In Proverbs 6, he tells us to get out of the trap of being responsible for another's debt (like co-signing on a loan) in the same way a gazelle would get away from a hunter or a bird would escape a snare[2]. He also encourages us to imitate the ant in order to avoid poverty by being productive and providing for the future. Agur in Proverbs 30 also speaks of creatures that are wise, though small: ants, locusts, coneys, and lizards[3].

When Jesus sent out his twelve disciples to spread the news of kingdom that was at hand, he told them to be wise as serpents but innocent as doves[4].

---

[1] The Random House College Dictionary, Revised Edition. (1988). New York, NY., Random House, Inc.
[2] All Biblical references come from the NIV Study Bible, New International Version. (1985). Grand Rapids, MI., Zondervan Bible Publishers.
[3] Proverbs 30:24-28
[4] Matthew 10:16

In order to really enjoy a dog, one doesn't merely try to train him to be semi human. The point of it is to open oneself to the possibility of becoming partly a dog." – Edward Hoagland[5]

There may be some objections to using animals as examples for people to follow. Some may ask, "Isn't their behavior just animal instinct, and not necessarily wisdom?" I believe that what we often pass off as "instinct" is in fact innate traits instilled *by* God, which means they show wisdom *from* God. My friend and minister Paul Shero often says about people who quit their jobs without having another one secured, "Even a monkey has enough sense to grab hold of one branch before he turns loose of another!"

Many psychologists agree that most of human behavior is not instinctual, but rather learned behavior. God has instilled innate wisdom in nature and some of that wisdom we would do well to learn from and imitate.

Another argument against looking to animals for examples to follow is that much of what an animal does is fixed pattern behavior in response to stimuli. In other words, they have little choice about their behavior – and can only do what they are preprogrammed by nature to do. For much of animal behavior and the survival instincts, this is true.

At the same time, the more complex the organism, the higher the sentient behavior as well. Animals can reason and think and choose behaviors that are not just instinctual response patterns. They can think, reason, and make choices.

---

[5] Retrieved September 5, 2010 from http://www.quotegarden.com/dogs.html

Dogs in particular can be wonderfully diverse in their behaviors and character.

Am I saying then that it would be better to be a creature with limited response pattern who has to do what it has been created to do, with little choice over its life? No, because no matter how smart they may be, animals are limited in their awareness of themselves and their surroundings. For example, my dog doesn't know that Paris, France even exists, nor will she ever.

When it comes to humans I don't think that God intended for us to be animal-like with a blind faith that was not reasoned out. We, as the pinnacle of God's creation[6], have the ability to make choices about our lives and our relationship with our Creator. That was a gift that God gave us – the freedom to choose whether or not to have a relationship with Him, and to choose how we will relate to others. This choice is what the leaders of the tribes of Israel challenged them to consider time and time again – to think out and choose their relationship with God[7].

Although humans have been given this gift of choice in our lives, we often make poor choices! Albert Einstein once commented, *"Only two things are finite, the universe and human stupidity, and I'm not sure about the former"*[8].

Can we learn to make better choices by observing the innate wisdom in nature? I think so! Animals show us God's wisdom by doing what they were created to do. In fact, God

---

[6] Genesis 1
[7] Deuteronomy 30:19; Joshua 24:15
[8] Albert Einstein. (n.d.). BrainyQuote.com. Retrieved August 22, 2010 from BrainyQuote.com Web site: http://www.brainyquote.com/quotes/quotes/a/alberteins100015.htm

created all of what we like to call outer space – the sun, moon, planets, stars, etc. – which glorify Him as well[9]. All of creation does what God created it to do.

What about us? What did he create *people* to do? Solomon lets us know that our duty is to *"Fear God, and keep His commandments, for this is the whole duty of man"*[10]. Why don't we do that? What keeps us from fulfilling our purpose like the rest of nature does?

I suspect that too often we forget what we were created for and we get sidetracked with the search for what will bring us comfort and pleasure in the here and now, our focus too much on the "seen" versus the "unseen"[11]. We could sure learn a lesson from nature in living our lives according to God's purposes for us. Well, in sum, that's the emphasis of this book.

On February 14 several years ago, my wife and I welcomed into our hearts and home an 8-week-old black Labrador Retriever puppy. She was soft, pudgy, and had those big ole paws that let you know that this dog has some growing up to do.

Right from the start we knew she was a special dog – she was bright, good-natured, and a bundle of energy! She has had indoor house privileges all of these years, and has slept beside our bed on her own mat. For some reason, she has decided to latch onto me as her special pal. Debra spends much more time with her and feeds her most of the time, but Sadie has attached herself to me, and she and I have been good buddies.

---

[9] Psalm 19:1-4
[10] Ecclesiastes 12:13
[11] 2 Corinthians 4:17-18

I have learned a lot about Labradors since owning Sadie, but more than that, I have learned a lot about my faith – or lack thereof – by observing her and her life. You see, I have come to realize that by watching nature, a person can have a deeper appreciation for God and His creation, and you can learn from nature the way in which a relationship with God should be developed and lived out. I have also come to realize that if I had half of the faith in God that my dog has in me, I would have a much better relationship with God.

So this little book is a compilation of some observations and insights into how, if I could be more like Sadie, I would have a closer walk with God. I hope that in reading it, you too can develop a closer relationship with, and confidence in, the One who created you and loves you deeply.

...I Would Do What I Was Created to Do!

"For we are God's workmanship, created in Christ Jesus to do good works..." Ephesians 2:10

What do Labrador Retrievers do? What's a distinctive trait of this type of dog? Well, the last part of the name is a dead giveaway: retriever. With Sadie, she is 100% Lab. When she gets up in the morning, the very first thing she does is to carry out of the room the little blanket she sleeps with. She also steals socks to carry them around, grabs my t-shirts, and runs around with them, picks up sticks in the yard and trots about, etc. It's just instinctive with her, and she is the happiest when she is carrying something in her mouth. The game of toss and retrieve is in her genes and she loves it.

When guests come over, she grabs a toy and parades around everyone, proudly showing them that she has something special in her mouth. It's just in her *nature* to want to retrieve and carry things in her mouth – and she's done it for over 13 years now.

Sadie is also by nature a bird-dog. She has always closely watched birds and taken a special interest in them. Her big ears square up on her head and her attention is riveted by watching birds. She delights in chasing them while on walks, and once in the backyard she caught a bird that was a little too slow getting away, and it didn't end well for the bird!

God has placed within her the instincts to behave in a certain fashion, and Sadie does just that. What about me? God has given me free will – the ability to choose my behavior, choose my path, and determine my own destiny, to some extent. But what is it that He has *created me* for? What is it that I should do?

Ecclesiastes 12 holds a part of the clue. When Solomon penned the words, *"Fear God, and keep His commandments"*[12], those words were written for me and you to help answer one of our deepest needs – to understand our purpose. Every person who has lived long enough to think rational thoughts has at some point asked themselves that very question: "What is *my* purpose? What is meaningful in life?"

So many voices pull at us to try to convince us that they will help to answer these questions and fill these needs. Advertisers constantly try to tap into our deepest desires for meaning and happiness, but the problem is that the promises they make offer just temporary fixes and insufficient answers. We're promised that the newest cell phone will somehow enhance our worthiness in the eyes of others, a flat-screen TV will make our lives now have meaning they didn't have before, and a new car will raise our self-esteem and value.

Max Weber, a famous sociologist in the 20th century, said that society is stratified by three major aspects: property, power, and prestige[13]. The more you have of those things, the higher your social status will be in the eyes of others. Dr. Paul Faulkner in his book *Making Things Right When Things Go Wrong*[14] points out that our society teaches that to have value and meaning in this life, we have to have at least some of the following qualities: athletic ability or some special talent, good looks, money, or intelligence. These will protect

---

[12] Ecclesiastes 12:13
[13] Weber, Max. (1991), "The Nature of Social Action", Runciman, W.G. *'Weber: Selections in Translation'*, Cambridge University Press.
[14] Faulkner, Paul. (1996). *Making Things Right When Things Go Wrong*. Howard Publishing Co.

you, give you meaning, and offer value to your life. At least that's what we're often being told on a daily basis through the mass media.

The message is: If you can run around a circle faster than anyone else can run around a circle, you're somebody! If you are good-looking, really pretty or handsome, you're somebody! If you have a lot of money, you are somebody! If you are really smart and have letters after your name, you're somebody!

But, as you probably suspect, these really offer little in the way of purpose or meaning. All of these things are short-term fixes for our self-worth and esteem. For instance, athletes can only compete for so long before their bodies are no longer able to do what younger players can do. Good looks will one day be replaced with wrinkles and other signs of aging – no matter what types of plastic surgery we have. Money can run out, and stock markets can lose money in a quick rush that leaves us financially on the edge. Alzheimer's or other forms of dementia can rob us of our intellectual abilities as well.

These solutions to self-esteem also only offer a temporary feeling of happiness. There have been people who have possessed some or all of these traits who have been miserable! In past years there were people like Marilyn Monroe and Howard Hughes, but in more recent times, icons such as Elvis Presley, Kurt Cobain, Michael Jackson, and scores of others, testify again and again that these traits do not equal enduring happiness.

Basing our self-worth on those qualities also sets us up for failure because they are largely out of our control. Circumstances play a major role in whether we ever have those socially desirable attributes or not. For instance, I could practice my basketball skills for 8 hours a day, and I will never be able to play in the NBA – *it's just not gonna happen!* A person's looks are based on their genes, and if you're ugly, there's not much you can do about that either! People who make money do so, not just because of hard work, but they also have to be in the right place at the right time for it to happen. In addition, there are many smart people out there who are not able to go to college and have degrees and letters behind their names, and their intelligence and ability is not recognized because of a lack of opportunity to further their education.

Now, if this was the only life that there was – and there was no life after death – then I would have to agree that the pursuit of whatever temporary fixes and pleasures in this life would be the ultimate purpose and meaning in life. Isn't that in fact what the apostle Paul argues when he writes, *"If the dead are not raised, 'Let us eat and drink, for tomorrow we die,'"*?[15]

Psychologists today are discovering that the quest for a fulfilling life does not lie in "pleasures", but rather in meaningful living. For instance, Martin Seligman in his book about positive psychology[16] notes that pleasures such as food, psychoactive substances (drugs), sex, and some work, are all shortcuts that bring about temporary fixes for happiness but leave the person desiring or wanting more.

Jesus also pointed out that centering our lives around things here on earth would be futile when He said, *"Do not*

---

[15] I Corinthians 15:32
[16] Seligman, Martin. (2002). *Authentic Happiness: Using the new positive psychology to realize your potential for lasting fulfillment.* New York, NY. The Free Press, Simon and Schuster, Inc.

store up for yourselves treasures on earth, where moth and rust destroy, and where thieves break in and steal"[17], and *"Do not work for food that spoils, but for food that endures to eternal life"*[18]. Things of this earth offer that temporary high, but ultimately lead to despair, disappointment, and disillusionment. They do not provide for us the purpose and meaning each one of us craves.

Perhaps Rick Warren said it best when he wrote, "You were shaped to serve God"[19]. I think those words echo the thoughts of Paul in Ephesians as he encouraged the believers to realize that they had a new nature to fulfill and new self to develop and live through[20]. Our life does not consist in the quest for possessions[21], power, or position, but rather in the meaningful work done in the name of Jesus to bring salvation to a lost and dying world, to alleviate human suffering when possible[22], and to conform ourselves to the image of Jesus[23].

This brings us back to the original question: What is *our* purpose and meaning in life? Again, Solomon wrote, *"Fear God, and keep His commandments."* These are the two basic purposes people have in life that can give it real meaning.

What does it mean to *"fear God"*? Although the word "fear" is translated in many ways, the basic meaning is to have a reverence and respect for God. Do you realize that life

---

[17] Matthew 6:19
[18] John 6:27
[19] Warren, Rick. (2002). *The Purpose Driven Life*. Grand Rapids, MI. Zondervan.
[20] Ephesians 4:22-24
[21] Luke 12:15
[22] Matthew 25:34-40
[23] Romans 8:29

without God is not possible? He is the one who sustains all of life with His word[24] - the rotation of the earth, the changing of the seasons, the air we breathe, and the food we have is all due to His sustaining power. Humans are really pretty frail creatures – it doesn't take much to destroy us, and even microorganisms can kill us! God, through His wisdom, sustains our very lives. There are those who believe that they have "made it" on their own merits, but they ignore the reality that *"the race is not to the swift or the battle to the strong, nor does food come to the wise or wealth to the brilliant or favor to the learned; but time and change happen to them all"*[25].

Additionally, and more importantly, He also sustains our very souls. Paul wrote to the Colossians[26] to tell us that God qualified us to share in His kingdom, something we can't do on our own. He rescued us from darkness – a vain, empty life – and He brought us into His kingdom. We were powerless to do anything to make up for our sins – those things we are ashamed of but can't go back and fix – and to be freed from them. God showed us His love when He sent Christ to provide for us a way to be free[27]. We don't have to live with the guilt and regret of the past. *What a blessing!* As a result, what do we owe God? All of our gratitude and respect - thus we reverence God.

The other part of what gives real meaning in life is to *"keep his commandments"*. We could, like the expert in the law who tried to test Jesus's credibility, work at making a list of laws and argue endlessly over which is most important and why. Jesus clearly ended that argument by stating that two

---

[24] Hebrews 1:3
[25] Ecclesiastes 9:11
[26] Colossians 1:12-13
[27] Romans 5:6-8

essential commandments form the foundation of one's faith: loving God with all one's heart and soul and mind, and loving our neighbor as ourselves[28].

So there we have it. The purpose for our lives is summed in trying to love God with all of our being (which would be evidenced by our thoughts, our devotion to Him, our finances, our choices, etc.), and caring for others as we care for ourselves (our families, co-workers, neighbors, those we find in need[29]). Both of these commandments are easy to say, but tough to do, given our tendency to put ourselves first.

Sadie does what she was created to do – and is 100% Lab through and through. It is much easier for her to do this – it is in her nature. What about you and me? Do you and I do what we were created to do? We have more choice over our lives than dogs do, yet at the same time we can aspire to participate in the divine nature that we were created for[30]. Paul wrote that *"we are God's workmanship, created in Christ Jesus to do good works"*[31].

One clear lesson that Sadie has taught me is that just as she is true to her nature as a retriever, I too should be true to my nature as a Christian. Although not easy, it is a worthy challenge to find real meaning in my life by living in a way that glorifies and honors my Creator. If I could be more like Sadie, I would do what I was created to do as well – *"Fear God, and keep His commandments."*

---

[28] Matthew 22:34-40
[29] Luke 10:27
[30] 2 Peter 1:4
[31] Ephesians 2:10

...I Wouldn't Bite!

"Be kind and compassionate to one another, forgiving each other, just as in Christ God forgave you." Ephesians 4:32

Ever been bitten by a wild animal? I'd like to say I haven't been, but unfortunately I was! When I was a junior in college and my younger brother was finishing his senior year in high school, he was a member of the club that took care of the mascot, the bobcat. Actually there were two bobcats that year that were the mascots: the wild one that was full-grown that stayed in a cage in the backyard, and a baby bobcat a rancher had found abandoned. We named the baby bobcat Bubba, and he was reared inside the house. He decided that he liked my room, and he chose to sleep in my bed with me every night. He was rambunctious and wild, and though affectionate, still had the wild tendencies in him.

One morning, while I was getting ready for church, Bubba got out of the bedroom where he was staying and ran into my mother's bedroom. I went in there, picked him up to carry him back to his part of the house, but he didn't want to go! Bubba proceeded to bite down on my wrist and buried his teeth in it. I yelled and dropped him as blood began to pour out of the holes he had made. He flattened his ears and leaped at my thigh and bit it too! I was able to herd him back into the part of the house where he was supposed to stay, and we stopped the bleeding, doctored my wounds, and headed to church. Needless to say, Bubba didn't sleep in my bed anymore – I didn't trust him! I still have a scar on my wrist where one of his fangs sunk deep into my skin.

Years later when Debra and I were taking time to choose the type of dog we wanted to have in our home, Labrador Retrievers sure fit the bill. We didn't want any dog that would be temperamental, fussy, or prone to snapping or biting when frustrated or angry. Especially since she is a big dog, that negative type of temperament could spell a nasty bite.

Now, of course, not all dogs fit their breed type exactly, and dogs can certainly vary in their overall disposition based on their biology and how they have been treated. In our case, Sadie is a typical Lab. She is as easy-going a dog as you will find. Although we know she really wouldn't ever hurt anyone intentionally, others don't know that. We've had contractors come to the house who were afraid to step inside the door because she is a big, black dog! She never acts in a hostile manner or snarls at anything or anyone, but given her size, she can be intimidating. Since we have had her, we have never had our house broken into – she's really a great theft deterrent without even having to try! Looks can be deceiving and in her case, they certainly are.

As she has gotten older, she's been affected by hip dysplasia, a condition in which the hip bone does not fit correctly into the socket. Even though she has joints that hurt and are painful, she doesn't get grouchy and bite when she moves around or when I have to pick her up to put her in the car for a vet visit.

When I compare Sadie's disposition with that of many people, I find a sharp contrast. Here looks can be deceiving, and sometimes they certainly are. Mark Twain once remarked, "If you pick up a starving dog and make him prosperous, he will not bite you. This is the principal difference between a dog and a man"[32]. People who at one

---

[32] Twain, M. Retrieved August 22, 2010 from http://www.quotationspage.com/quote/354.html

moment are smiling and seemingly cheerful can turn in a split second like a pit viper and strike.

For example, sometimes stress puts people in a mood to bite others. Ever been shopping around Christmas? People who supposedly are celebrating the birth of Christ and thinking about God's love towards them also think nothing about cutting you off when you are trying to buy something they have their eye on. The same thing is true when driving as well. For 10 years we have lived close to interstates. Talk about road rage and mean drivers! People get so upset and drive offensively, not defensively, and use creative hand signals to communicate with you.

Sadly, when I compare Sadie's disposition with that of some of my fellow Christians, I too find a sharp contrast. Here again looks can be deceiving, and sometimes they certainly are. Some of the most mean-spirited people I have met were professing Christians. In appearance, they dress the part, come to worship faithfully, give their money to the church, partake of the Lord's Supper, pray, sing, etc., but if one thing doesn't go their way, they will snap and bite your head off!

Introduce a new song into the worship service and watch out – you'll get bit! Ask a bible class teacher to allow another teacher to teach in their place for a quarter and you might see "bared teeth"! Accidentally sit in "someone's pew" as a visitor and you might get an earful. Ask a question in bible class and get ridiculed or putdown by those "who are more knowledgeable". Some of these may seem like examples that are unbelievable but I've witnessed them all and have been "bitten" myself a number of times.

Sometimes Christians bite because they don't like change. The known is so much more comfortable, and rather than having to think or do anything different, they snap at others and growl and complain in an attempt to keep things the same. I'm not talking about doctrinal changes which are another matter entirely, but rather changes in simple worship services. This biting can either be an attempt to be in charge or just to object to anything that is different.

Looking back now, I realize that to expect a wild bobcat to behave like a domesticated animal is unrealistic. At the time, Bubba's aggression certainly was a painful surprise, but I should have anticipated that type of behavior might happen. After all, he was a wild animal! Also, expecting people who are not Christians to act and respond like Christians is unrealistic too. They may be temperamental, selfish, greedy, etc., but that's the kind of behavior one might expect from a person who has never named the name of Christ and is being transformed by His power.

In addition, we live in a culture in which witty, cutting remarks are seen as marks of a quick mind. The ability to snap back at someone with a retort is viewed with respect and shows an ability to defend oneself or one's position. In addition, comedians become popular by spouting one-liners that are acerbic and biting. So our very culture encourages people to speak their mind no matter who may get hurt in the process – it's our first amendment right, isn't it?

Within the body of believers though, I think it is right to expect a *different* type of behavior. I'm not saying that people should be perfect, and we are all sinners struggling to become like Jesus. At the same time, we need to be aware of just how devastating "biting" can be to the church. Paul sends out a clear warning to the Galatian believers when he wrote, *"The entire law is summed up in a single command:*

'Love your neighbor as yourself.' If you keep on biting and devouring each other, watch out or you will be destroyed by each other"[33].

The question that comes to us is, "Where does this biting behavior come from?" Paul gives us one clue further on in chapter 5 of Galatians, when he pens, *"Let us not become conceited, provoking and envying each other."*[34] Pride, the desire to be first, and the desire to have one's own way, often becomes the motivation for biting remarks that cut to the soul. Having lost the humility that brings about the gratitude for one's salvation, a person may become comfortable with their faith and feel a sense of entitlement that allows them to react to others in a hateful manner. Neglecting their own need to continue to grow in the fruits of the Spirit[35], their tolerance for others winds up falling by the wayside, and words are spoken that destroy faith. Perhaps this is what Solomon meant when he wrote, *"The tongue has the power of life and death..."*[36] Solomon also penned, *"Reckless words pierce like a sword..."*[37], and I've known people whose biting remarks have caused others to lose their faith, give up on God, and while bleeding, turn from the church.

So what's the solution? I think perhaps going back to the basics. Jesus said that the basics are: Love your God with all your heart, soul, mind, and strength, and love your neighbor as yourself[38]. Easy words to say, but tough, tough words to live out in our everyday lives. Rather than thinking

---

[33] Galatians 5:14-15
[34] Galatians 5:25
[35] Galatians 5:22-23
[36] Proverbs 18:21
[37] Proverbs 12:18
[38] Mark 12:28-31

that we should have our way and our say, Jesus calls us to serve others and to consider them first[39].

How about working on this as well: following the words of Paul when he wrote, *"Do not let any unwholesome talk come out of your mouths, but only what is helpful for building others up according to their needs, that it may benefit those who listen"*[40]. Rather than snipping and biting to get our way, we could instead think about the impact of our words on the hearer. Putting their needs before our own, we could stop short of saying things that condemn, that hurt, and that discourage others and cause untold damage. I guess it basically comes back to considering others better than ourselves, and acting and speaking accordingly[41]. *"Let your conversation be always full of grace, seasoned with salt, so that you may know how to answer everyone"*[42].

Wild animals may bite; that's what they do. People who are not Christians may bite too; that's what they do. Sadie didn't bite back though, even with provocation, and I don't think Christians should bite either! If I could be more like Sadie, I wouldn't snap at others, I would be more careful with what I say, and I would be more easygoing in my disposition. It's like the little boy who prayed, "Lord, make all the bad people good, and all the good people nice."

Let's make an agreement to stop the snarling, quit baring our fangs, and take on a gentle, humble nature among the people in the body of Christ we are a part of, and among the people in the world as well. Who knows? Maybe they'll even think we're friendly!

---

[39] Mark 10:42-45
[40] Ephesians 4:29
[41] Philippians 2:3-4
[42] Colossians 4:6

"The reason a dog has so many friends is he wags his tail instead of his tongue." – Anonymous

...I Would Have No Worries!

"Do not be anxious about anything, but in everything, by prayer and petition, with thanksgiving, present your requests to God." Philippians 4:6

    Sadie has to be one of the most laid-back dogs you'll ever meet. Talk about contentment: she has all of her needs and most of her wants taken care of! Twice a day her food bowl is filled with food. (It doesn't last though but a few moments before it's down the hatch!) Her water bowl is continually filled with good, clean water. She goes out to explore the backyard whenever she asks to, for the most part, and she lives in an air-conditioned and heated home. She gets to go on two walks a day to scope out the neighborhood.

    Sadie also has two beds: one in the kitchen where she likes to lie down while Debra is preparing meals (just in case some food accidentally hits the floor), and one in the bedroom at night for her to sleep on. These orthopedic beds give relief to her sore joints and help her to relax and feel better.

    Now, does Sadie worry about dog food prices and how much it costs? No way – she is blissfully ignorant of that. She is unaware of veterinarian's bills and costs of medications. She doesn't worry about whether or not she's taken her vitamin supplements, whether it is going to rain this next weekend, etc. Sadie is aging, but she doesn't worry about her appearance or the fact that she's slowed down a bit. All she does is live and enjoy the benefits of her master's care. All that she needs is taken care of, and she doesn't worry with the details of how that is accomplished.

    What about me? Well, it's easy to worry, isn't it? With stock markets going down, the price of oil going up, the changing job markets, globalization, and rapid changes in technology that leave one wondering if they can keep up, etc., there seems to be a lot to worry about! It seems every other week some new health discovery is trying to convince us that we need to eat some other type of food or swallow some other type of vitamins/supplements so that we won't age as fast and can keep looking as good as possible for as long as possible. We not only worry about our house, car, jobs, and appearance, but we also worry about what others think about our house, car, jobs, and appearance. Whew! That's a lot to worry about too!

In the midst of our anxiousness about life and the future, the Master's calm words speak to us about His care for us. In Matthew 6 Jesus comforts and encourages His followers by saying that God the Father takes care of the plants and the birds, and we are more valuable than they are! He promises that our physical needs will be provided for, so we should really have no worries! Our focus should be on seeking His kingdom and righteousness[43].

Well, what about the future when I die? Shouldn't I at least be concerned about that? Jesus said that those who follow Him should not be troubled by this either, because a place in heaven has been prepared for us[44]. As long as we are walking in the light[45], there is no condemnation for those in Christ[46] and death is not something to be feared[47].

If those promises are true, why then am I anxious? It really all comes down to what or who you trust in. What are

---

[43] Matthew 6:25-34
[44] John 14:1-3
[45] 1 John 1:7
[46] Romans 8:1-2
[47] 1 Corinthians 15:50-58

some of the people or things we are tempted to trust in? One is money and possessions. If you trust in money, then the stock market's movements will make you anxious because it is not stable and certain. If you trust in possessions to make you somebody or to give you a sense of certainty, you will be anxious because nothing is certain about our "things". What was it again that Jesus said about worldly treasures? Rust happens, moths happen, and thieves may want to steal your stuff[48]!

Another thing we may trust in is our own health, appearance, or physical strength. But age will rob you little by little of those things – no matter what drugs you take or surgery you have. Steroids, Botox, and plastic surgery can only do so much. You will get weaker, have more wrinkles, not be as "attractive" by the world's standards, and your body will wear out – that's the plain, unvarnished truth.

We may be tempted to trust in our own intelligence. But if you trust in your own ability to think and figure things out, your wisdom will fail you because not everyone can be smart about everything. You will always be vulnerable to making errors and possibly major mistakes in judgment in areas that are not familiar to you. I've known many people who were "book smart" but lacked the ability to connect with people. They suffered in their personal relationships because they didn't have "people smarts" to interact with others. Additionally, age will cause a slowing of the ability to reason as quickly and effectively. A person should get wisdom with age, but a wise person also knows that they don't know everything!

---

[48] Matthew 6:19-21

What about trusting others? Well, if you trust in other people, they will disappoint you. No one is perfect, and even those closest to us will sometimes hurt us or let us down with things they say or do. Whether purposeful or accidental, pain is a part of human relationships. Jesus knew that people should not be His source of strength or trust, so He kept Himself from fully relying on others[49]. Even death separates us, at least for a while, from our loved ones. Either they leave us, or we leave them, but the end result is the same – a sense of loneliness and loss. Trusting in someone else to always be there for us and to never disappoint us sets us up to be anxious.

What then is the remedy for anxiety and worry? Trust. Not in money, looks, intelligence, others, nor your own strength and abilities, but rather trust in God. God has said, *"Never will I leave you, never will I forsake you"*[50]. In fact, nothing can separate us from the love that God has for us in Christ Jesus[51]. Jesus said, *"Do not let your hearts be troubled. Trust in God; trust also in me"*[52].

This trust is reflected in our willingness to go to God with the things we need help with. Paul wrote that instead of being anxious, we could go to God in prayer about everything and leave with a sense of peace that would guard our hearts and minds[53].

Are we talking about an easy life with no hardships? Of course not – that's unrealistic to expect. What we are talking about is the ability to not be anxious about what may

---

[49] John 2:23-25
[50] Hebrews 13:5
[51] Romans 8:35-39
[52] John 14:1
[53] Philippians 4:6-8

happen in this temporary, changing, and chaotic world we live in. We have a God who loves us, who provides our basic needs, who doesn't change, and who will be there for us in this life and the next life. Trusting in that truth can be a real antidote for anxiety!

Sadie doesn't worry about her needs being met because she has a loving master who anticipates her needs and takes care of her. If I could be more like Sadie and trust that my Master anticipates my needs and takes care of me too, I would have no worries as well!

"I think we are drawn to dogs because they are the uninhibited creatures we might be if we weren't certain we knew better. They fight for honor at the first challenge, make love with no moral restraint, and they do not for all their marvelous instincts appear to know about death. Being such wonderfully uncomplicated beings, they need us to do their worrying." – George Bird Evans[54]

---

[54] Retrieved September 5, 2010 from http://www.quotegarden.com/dogs.html

...I Would Forgive More Easily!

"Bear with each other and forgive whatever grievances you may have against one another. Forgive as the Lord forgave you." Colossians 3:13

Most psychologists agree that a major problem between people – whether it is a marriage, family relationship, friendship, or nations – is the lack of forgiveness. Holding onto grudges – how easy it is to do! Someone offends us, hurts us, and we don't forget easily. Hurts and wounds, if untreated, grow into grudges and hatred, which can lead to violence, child abuse, wars, and even apathy. We often wait until the other person has in some way acknowledged their wrong before we are even willing to consider forgiving. "They should have known better," we think.

Our Lab Sadie is different than that. She is not a dog who carries a grudge. Of course she does have good care provided, but we aren't perfect. Sadie is fed first thing in the morning, usually about 6:00am, and then again at 4:00pm. There are times though when Debra and I are gone and are not able to get back by 4:00pm to feed her. As a matter of fact, sometimes it is 2-3 hours later when we get home. When we come through the door, she doesn't give us a condescending look or snub our affection because we were way over time for getting her supper to her. She is just glad to see us – let bygones be bygones – and eat!

There are times, when frustrated, I will yell at her to get out of the way (she is prone to walking right in front of me and stopping abruptly where I almost trip over her). She doesn't have the problem – I do – but she doesn't slink off and sulk and wait for me to apologize. She is ready for us to be friends again instantly. In fact, when I do apologize and give her a big hug or pat on the head, she is good to go – no harm done. The dog doesn't carry a grudge. Whatever was in the past was in the past, and she is ready to move on.

What about us? We usually are not quite so fast to forgive others. We hold onto grudges and nurture them, going over and over in our minds the hurtful things that were said or done. One cartoon I read once had the main character saying, *"Holding onto a grudge ain't such a bad thing...it sharpens your memory,"* and there are a lot of people with "sharp" memories!

Lewis Smedes in his book, *Forgive and Forget*, talks about how hard it can be at times to forgive someone who has hurt us[55]. There are a myriad of reasons why we may be reluctant to forgive one another. We may be tempted to not forgive easily because sometimes we can be mean-spirited. Paul wrote Titus to tell him that before Christ *"we lived in malice and envy, being hated and hating one another"*[56]. We have to work to put that kind of mindset away.

We also may not want to forgive because we lose a focus of attention. We are no longer a "victim" and can't hold that power over someone else. We may believe that forgiveness equals tolerance and the offense won't mean very much (when in actuality, the very reason we are forgiving someone is because a real offense has occurred that cannot be tolerated). Or perhaps we think that some kind of justice should occur, and forgiveness means that we have to give up getting even or settling the score in some manner. A sense of

---

[55] Smedes, Lewis, (2007). *Forgive and Forget: Healing the Hurts We Don't Deserve.* HarrperOne Publishing.
[56] Titus 3:3

fairness cries out for revenge! Paul though told the Corinthians to *"not take revenge, my friends..."*[57]

What is forgiveness? Smedes believes it is an "ought" that flows from who we are. Just as dogs ought to bark, birds ought to fly, Christians "ought" to forgive. That was the point of Jesus' parable in Matthew 18 about the unforgiving servant. What sticks out so vividly in that story is the servant's unwillingness to recognize the great debt he had been forgiven, and to pass that blessing onto another. He missed it! Paul writes that grace for our sins is a gift from God[58], and as we seek to model ourselves after Jesus[59], we too should be forgivers of others.

Both Jesus and Paul elevate this forgiveness to a high level – it is really not an option in the Christian life. Jesus said, *"For if you forgive men when they sin against you, your heavenly Father will also forgive you. But if you do not forgive men their sins, your Father will not forgive your sins"*[60]. Our own forgiveness is intimately and intricately tied in with our willingness to forgive others. Paul goes on to write, *"Be kind and compassionate to one another, forgiving each other, just as in Christ God forgave you"*[61].

How does one "do" forgiveness? There is no simple formula, and it is one of the most difficult things a person does as a Christian. Here are three suggestions that may make forgiveness an easier task to achieve.

First, focus *on your own forgiveness.* The writer of Hebrews expresses it this way: *"See to it that no one misses*

---

[57] Romans 12:19
[58] Ephesians 2:8
[59] Romans 8:29
[60] Matthew 6:14-15
[61] Ephesians 4:32

the grace of God and that no bitter root grows up to cause trouble and defile many"[62]. If you miss God's grace and forget to focus on it, then it is easy to become a bitter person who doesn't forgive. When you consider the great debt of sin that God has freely released you from, as far as the east is from the west[63], it becomes much easier to forgive someone for the things they have done to you. If the parable that Jesus told in Matthew 18 is any gauge, there are few times that the offense someone commits against us comes anywhere close to the magnitude of the offenses from which God has forgiven us[64].

Second, you have to *see the person who offended you or who hurt you as God sees them: A needy person trying to meet their needs in some sinful way.* All of us are confusing admixtures of good and evil – just ask Paul[65]. Even Hitler, as cruel as he was, was kind to his dog!

So all of us at times can be good to others and not so good as well. We all struggle with blind spots and are able to see the sins of others much more clearly than we see or discern our own sins. We tell ourselves, "They are awful people" when someone hurts us, but when we hurt someone else, we are remarkably good at making up excuses for why we did or said the things we did. "I was just joking!", "I was having a bad day," "they are too sensitive," or "I was just telling the truth," etc. We too can hurt others, sometimes unknowingly, and not be our best either.

Rather than making those who have sinned against us out to be monsters, perhaps it would be better to view them

---

[62] Hebrews 12:15
[63] Psalm 103:11-12
[64] Matthew 18:21-35
[65] Romans 7:14-15

as weak and needy, much like ourselves. God sees everyone as people who need to be saved[66], and He was willing to send His Son to die for us *"while we were still sinners..."*[67] Paul writes that as believers we need to begin to see people in a different way, as God does[68]. Seeing others in this way does not mean that a sin or offense hasn't occurred. God, even though seeing us as sinful and powerless, still needed to send Jesus to take care of our sin problem. In the same way, seeing others who hurt us as weak doesn't excuse the sin, but it may make it easier for us to forgive them.

Third, *remember the freedom that forgiving another gives to you.* Jesus' teaching illustrates clearly that unforgiving persons always wind up in prison[69], and what imprisons us is our own resentments, anger, memories of a painful past, and depression. Forgiveness releases us from a painful past. Phil McGraw in his book, *Life Strategies*, believes that by forgiving another we are able to avoid being tied to someone by a painful past. He writes that the forgiving person is in essence saying, "I will not allow you to drag me into your dark world. By forgiving you, I am releasing me..."[70] The person who forgives gets the freeing from the past first! This area of forgiveness is in the "deep end" of the swimming pool of our faith. It is not an easy task to accomplish, especially when we have been hurt in some way.

Jesus taught there was one additional way to deal with others who have sinned against us, and that is to pray

---

[66] 2 Peter 3:9
[67] Romans 5:6-8
[68] 2 Corinthians 5:16
[69] Matthew 18:34
[70] McGraw, Phil. (1999). *Life Strategies: Doing what works, doing what matters.* New York, NY: Hyperion, p. 205.

for them[71]. If we pray for them and wish them well, we are actually imitating the Father and being like Him, who treats all people with equal concern. Ask yourself, "Doesn't the person who wronged us need our prayers?" The answer is, "Yes, they sure do." When we pray for our offender, we gradually lose the desire to see bad things happen to them.

Again, forgiveness is a tough challenge, and Christianity is not for those who want an easy life – it's hard! Some tough questions arise when we talk about forgiveness. I don't propose to have all of the answers, but here are some things to think about. Tough question number one: *"Does forgiveness mean reconciliation?"* The answer is, *"Sometimes, but not always."* The forgiven person can be inside the circle of people we pray about, but not necessarily back in our close circle of friends or family. Think about a child molester, an employee who steals your money, or an adulterous spouse. We can forgive even if we do not trust the other person, but we can be reconciled only if we can trust that the person who wronged us will not do that again. One of the consequences of sin may be a loss of relationship. The Jewish tribes who rebelled against God by not wanting to go on into the Promised Land were forgiven, but they would not see the land that God had prepared for them[72]. Similarly, the Jewish nation under King Josiah had made great strides in turning around the nation from the idolatry and wickedness it had been involved in. Yet, Manasseh's sins had been so great that God would not turn away from His wrath and the ultimate overthrow and captivity of the nation[73].

---

[71] Matthew 5:44-18
[72] Numbers 14:20-23
[73] 2 Kings 23:21-23; 24:2

Two barriers go up between people when a person is wronged. One barrier is on our side, and our willingness to forgive removes it. The other barrier is on the side of the offender, and it can only be worked on by them through repentance[74] and restitution[75].

Tough question number two: *"Does forgiveness mean I have to tolerate bad behavior?"* The answer is, *"No."* When discussing forgiveness, Peter's question to Jesus showed a legalistic way of showing forgiveness[76]. Jesus' response was basically to say, "Don't be a scorekeeper – keeping tabs on one's forgiveness is not a merciful thing to do."

We do, however, need to set limits on tolerance, which is different from forgiveness. In the Sermon on the Mount, Jesus talked about being mistreated and our response to abuse by others. He said we should *"turn the other cheek," "let him have our cloak as well,"* and *"go with him two miles"*[77]. But Jesus didn't say, "let them beat you to a pulp, give them all your possessions, and walk one-hundred miles". He was encouraging His followers to go beyond what revenge or retaliation might suggest we do, and instead bear up under unfair circumstances. Does that mean we tolerate unfair circumstances when we don't have to? I don't think so. Paul sure didn't think so either, and he used his Roman citizenship to not only convict the consciences of those who had unjustly beaten and imprisoned him[78], but to also avoid being flogged without a trial[79]. We can forgive others who

---

[74] Luke 17:3-4
[75] Luke 19:8
[76] Matthew 18:21-23
[77] Matthew 5:38-42
[78] Acts 16:32-40
[79] Acts 22:22-29

have wronged us, but that does not mean we have to put ourselves in a position to be wronged again and again and be forced to tolerate sinful behavior.

Tough question number three: *"If I can't forget it, does that mean I haven't forgiven it?"* The answer is, *"No."* Paul, when writing the Corinthian believers, rattled off a long list of psychological and physical torment he had been through because of others[80]. He had not forgotten what had happened to him, any more than a person who has suffered some serious injury forgets the physical pain that they had at the time of the injury. The difference is what we are focusing on. Paul didn't spend time focusing on his painful experiences, but rather spent his time focusing ahead to the "unseen" eternal realities[81], and because of that he did not lose heart. We too can choose either to dwell on the wounds, the unfairness, the abuse, the cruelty, and the wrongs we've endured at the hands of others, or focus on what is in our future – an eternal glory where sin does not exist.

Tough question number four: *"Can you forgive someone who doesn't ask for it?"* The answer is, *"Yes."* Jesus modeled that for us on the cross when He said, *"Father, forgive them, for they do not know what they are doing"*[82]. Sometimes we have no other option but to forgive someone who hasn't asked for it because they are deceased. We may have to write down the hurts that someone has caused us, pray about it, and then release it.

We can forgive, or at least do our part in forgiving another person, but it really can't be complete without the other person working on their side of the barrier. That's the

---

[80] 2 Corinthians 11:23-27
[81] 2 Corinthians 4:16-18
[82] Luke 23:24

situation Jesus spoke of when he told his followers, *"If your brother sins, rebuke him, and if he repents, forgive him"*[83]. The other side of this situation would ask, "What if the person doesn't repent? What if they really don't care that they have hurt us, or they see nothing wrong with what they did or said?" We can only work on our side of the barrier. We can do our part with forgiving another person, even if they don't ask for it, but for forgiveness to be complete, the person who sins against us must be willing to acknowledge that hurt and repent.

    Forgiving others: A real challenge for Christians who want to walk in the steps of the Savior. Sadie forgives easily and holds no grudges – she just looks past the offense and is ready to move on. If I could be more like Sadie, I too would forgive more easily, focus on the "unseen", and move on too. The rearview mirror in the car is small for a reason – it should be considered, but it is not the direction we are driving in! We should be looking out the front windshield where we are going. In the same way, we can use our past and the things that have happened to us as a reference point, but our focus should be on what's ahead and the promises God has waiting for us in eternity. I'm ready to look ahead – how about you?

"Dog's lives are too short. Their only fault, really."
    – *Agnes Sligh Turnbull*[84]

---

[83] Luke 17:3
[84] Retrieved September 5, 2010 from http://www.quotegarden.com/dogs.html

...I Would Find My Master's Presence Comforting!

"When I am afraid, I will trust in you" Psalm 56:3

West Texas thunderstorms – often a very welcome sight! In a region that doesn't get much rain, the sight of an approaching storm means some relief from the heat and some much welcome rain for the land. These storms can be dangerous though with the weather phenomenon they create. One evening Debra and I were at a friend's house when a West Texas thunderstorm came in. You know the type: bright flashes of lightning, thunder that sounds like a rifle shot, high winds, heavy rain that's blinding, and hail. Now Sadie usually stays out when we're gone for a while, and she not only has a good doghouse, but her house was up on a porch where neither rain, hail, nor wind could affect it. So she was protected from the weather just fine. Nevertheless, when we finally made it home after the storm, she was traumatized. The lightning and thunder had really taken their toll on her nerves, and she was upset. We let her back in the house, sat with her, and petted her while she calmed down from the event.

Ever since then, when a storm comes up and thunder begins to roll, she gets nervous. If she is by herself or off in another room, she gets antsy. But if she can find me, she comes to where I am, lies down, and then gets very calm and goes to sleep. Now the thunder is still going on, and of course I am powerless to stop it, but she finds that being with me is comforting, and she feels just fine as long as she is with me.

Sadie's shown this lack of fear when I'm around at other times as well. Once my father-in-law, who was visiting at the time, bought a leaf blower for us to use to clear off our really long driveway that would get covered again and again by leaves in the fall. I was at work at the time, and when he fired it up, Sadie didn't like it very much and was skittish around it. When I came home, Debra said that her father had bought the leaf blower, but that Sadie didn't like it. She was concerned that we might not be able to use it around her. I went in the garage and got the leaf blower out and began using it with Sadie in the yard to see how she would react. The result? No reaction at all! If I was using it, she didn't have any fear of it – she is the same way with the lawn mower as well. It's as if she knows that if something is in my hands, I will not let it harm her.

    On another occasion she was chewing on one of her chew-toys when her teeth broke through a part of the toy and her lip got pinched in the opening. She jumped up yelping because she couldn't get it off and it was tightly pinching her lip! I ran out and got a pair of pliers and while Debra held her, I pried it apart and removed the toy from her lip. The whole time I was doing this, she stayed very calm and patient.

    When we go on walks, she sometimes gets goat-head stickers in her paws (there's a lot of those sticker weeds in West Texas!). When our little dog Bo would get these stickers, we would try to pull them out, but the whole time he was snarling and upset, as if we were the ones who stuck them in his paws to begin with! Sadie though just stops, lifts up her paw, and waits patiently as I remove the sticker. Although it hurts her for me to do this, she trusts that I will relieve her of the pain of the goat-head.

    You see, Debra and I made sure that we never hit or harmed Sadie with our hands. We wanted her to not fear our hands or our touch. Haven't you seen dogs who shy away when you reach to pet them? Often that is a result of a dog who's been hit and who has learned to be cautious. The presence of a person's hands is not comforting, but rather fearful.

Also, whenever I take her anywhere, she is ready to go! She doesn't have a clue where she's going – on a short trip to get a Coke, on a long trip to visit relatives, or a trip to the vet. As long as I am going somewhere, she wants to go along too! She loves to do the dog thing and hang her head out the window, soaking in all the sights and smells of whatever journey we're on.

Could I find my Master's presence as comforting? I should. Paul describes God as *"the Father of compassion and the God of all comfort..."*[85] As I reflect on the word of God, isn't that what God has been trying to do with His followers all along? He comforted Abram, Isaac, and Jacob when they were travelers in a foreign land. He comforted the tribes of Israel and led them out of captivity in a foreign land, making it clear that He was with them by the sight of the pillar of fire at night and the pillar of cloud by day. He actually had them set up a place for Him to be in their presence, the tabernacle, where they could always know that God was with them. When His Son came to earth, His name was *"God with us"*[86], and the last thing that Jesus told His followers was that He would always be with them[87]. God has made it abundantly clear that He wants to be in the presence of His followers.

Now, that presence can be upsetting if we have things in our lives that we don't want to face God with. Take the example of Cain, how he skirted the sin he had committed

---

[85] 2 Corinthians 1:3
[86] Matthew 1:23
[87] Matthew 28:20

and tried to dodge God regarding the murder of his brother[88]. On the other hand, that presence can be comforting if we believe and have confidence that God seeks to cover our sins[89] if we will come into His presence and confess them.

 I think that God's presence should not only bring about a peace within us because our sins are forgiven[90], but it should bring about an awareness of what we are doing and thinking. Have you ever been with a small child watching television and then realized how inappropriate the program was for the child to see? The presence of the child causes us to "see" things differently through their eyes and do things differently as well.

 We are more aware of potential dangers they could get into, as well as more things that they would get enjoyment out of. Recently as we traveled in Laramie, Wyoming, we saw a 6 ft. dinosaur, a brontosaurus I think, outside of a Sinclair gasoline station. Normally that would not have been anything much to pay attention to, but because we have a 4 year old niece, Kaitlyn, who is excited about dinosaurs, I knew that she would get a kick out of me having my picture made beside it. Debra took the picture of me petting the dinosaur, I wrote a note and enclosed the picture along with it in a letter to Kaitlyn, and she was delighted to get it in the mail. Not only was it fun for her to get mail, but especially of her uncle petting a dinosaur!

 In the same way, if we are aware of God's presence, we will also "see" things and people differently and do things differently. Years ago a popular bracelet had on it "WWJD" – "What Would Jesus Do?" to remind the wearer of God's

---

[88] Genesis 4:1-12
[89] Psalm 32:1-2
[90] Romans 5:1

influence on our choices. It's not just the avoidance of things that would be sinful, but also the awareness of things that would please God. Hopefully we will also be aware of things that will bring Him joy as well: opportunities for service to Him, to others, to pray, to give thanks, etc. In fact, Paul encourages the Ephesian believers to *"find out what pleases the Lord"*[91].

I heard a story once about two men who were Christians and best friends, one of whom was a doctor. One night, as the one friend was ill and near death, his friend who was a doctor came to see him. The doctor had brought his dog with him, but left him outside of the room when he went in to see his ailing friend. The man who was ill expressed his fear of dying and what would happen after death. The doctor sat beside him for an hour, comforting him as he listened to his friend talk about his fears. Finally the doctor told his friend, "Ever since I have been in here with you, my dog has scratched at the door and begged to be in here. He has never been in this room before, and knows nothing about it. All he knows is that through this door his master is in here, and he wants to be with me. As long as he's with me, he is all right. You're going to be going through a door to a place that you've never been before, and you know little about what's on the other side of death's door. But your Master is there, and as long as you are with him, you will be all right."

That reminds me of the old song, *"Anywhere with Jesus"*, that expresses so well the thought that in the Master's presence, we are safe. Two oft cited ways of being in the Master's presence are by prayer and reading His word. Prayer should be like breathing to us, a natural phenomenon that gives us life. Jesus has promised us that if we ask, He

---

[91] Ephesians 5:10

will answer. I don't believe that God is ever closer to us than when we talk with Him from our hearts.

Additionally, His word was not left to us to be dry, stale, and boring, but rather to be living words that give us confidence and hope. By reading it, we can see God's movement not only in the lives of those who followed Him in the past, but also we can find assurances of His presence and His working in our lives today. Peter says that God has given us *"...his very great and precious promises..."*[92] Every time we open His word, we are being invited into His presence, to a special relationship and communication with Him.

If I could be more like Sadie, I would find peace in my Master's presence and would find being with Him very comforting. I would also be ready to go with Him anywhere!

---

[92] 2 Peter 1:4

...I Would Enjoy People More!

"This is the message you have heard from the beginning: We should love one another." I John 4:11

Labrador Retrievers have the reputation of being friendly and kind, and good with children. In fact, the website of the American Kennel Club describes these dogs as "gentle, intelligent and family-friendly"[93]. They go on to say that with regard to a Lab's temperament, "The ideal disposition is one of a kindly, outgoing, tractable nature; eager to please and non-aggressive towards man or animal. The Labrador has much that appeals to people; his gentle ways, intelligence and adaptability make him an ideal dog."

Sadie fits the bill with friendliness as far as Labradors go. When she meets someone, she assumes they want to meet her too! It starts with her big tail, and then soon her whole body is shaking back and forth and she gets excited over meeting people. She always thinks people are neat and has no preconceived notions about them – she just thinks they all are cool.

She started to smile at people as well when she was about 5 years old. Have you ever seen a dog "smile"? It isn't particularly pretty, but she does it. The first time she did it was in the veterinarian's office. It sort of looked like a snarl with her upper lips pulled back and her teeth showing. Of course, a big dog with big teeth showing can look menacing! What gave her away was the whole body shaking thing. The vet said, "Look, she's smiling!" and went on to explain that some dogs actually smile at people. Somehow Sadie has added this to her "meet and greet" repertoire, which includes

---

[93] American Kennel Club – www.akc.org

the tail whip, the body shake, and carrying around something in her mouth like she is in a parade. She began smiling more and more at new people she would encounter, and we would just laugh at her appearance and antics. Everything about her just says, *"I am so happy to meet you!"* She sees in every person the potential for a friend who wants to pet her and get to know her. Norman Strung remarked, *"Labradors [are] lousy watchdogs. They usually bark when there is a stranger about, but it is an expression of unmitigated joy at the chance to meet somebody new, not a warning"*[94].

Although Sadie is that way toward people, I must confess that the same is not so much true with me. I tend to be more on the introverted side of the personality scale. I don't harbor prejudices that I am aware of toward others and I don't dislike people. In fact, I get along with almost everyone with no problems – I'm just fine with a little contact and I enjoy many times working alone.

By contrast, in reading the Bible I am struck by two main movements of God with regard to people. One is His attempt to get as close to them as possible. Have you noticed this? A popular song years ago talked about God watching us from a distance, and when I hear that song I am reminded of just how wrong that part of the song is theologically. Rather than being an unfeeling God who is distant and removed from people, He very much wants to be in the midst of them.

Start off in the garden. We find God, having newly created the world, enjoying walking with man there. Adam and Eve's sin broke that fellowship, and the rest of the Bible is a chronicle of God's working to bring people back into a close relationship with Him. He appears and talks with the

---

[94] www.dogquotations.com

patriarchs: Abram, Isaac, and Jacob. He delivers His people from cruel slavery they were suffering under in Egypt. He leads them in the wilderness by showing them His constant presence in a cloud by day and a pillar of fire by night. He instructs the Israelites to fashion a portable tent, called the tabernacle, as a place for Him to dwell among them in the center of the tribes. In the land He promised to bring them to, He had Solomon build a temple into which His glory would come down – and it was to be a visual reminder of His presence.

Even more amazing was the fact that God actually came down, became a person, and walked among people in order to be close to them. The first chapter of John talks about this amazing event and reports, *"The Word became flesh and made his dwelling among us"*[95]. The name that people would call Jesus, *"Immanuel"*, was a fulfillment of what Isaiah had centuries earlier said would happen, and that name means, *"God with us"*[96].

Jesus then provided a way for followers of God to be cleansed from their sins, and upon believing and being baptized into His name, part of God lives inside of each and every believer[97]. Paul makes this clear to the Corinthians when he encourages them to realize that our physical body is actually a temple of the Holy Spirit[98]. God lives inside of us! This quest of God to be close to His people was once again made possible through the atonement for our sins through the sacrifice and blood of Jesus[99]. Jesus' last words to his

---

[95] John 1:14
[96] Matthew 1:23
[97] Acts 2:38
[98] I Corinthians 6:18-20
[99] Hebrews 10

disciples were, *"And surely I am with you always, to the very end of the age"*[100].

This phenomenon of a God wanting to be close to His people is singularly found in the true God. Pagan gods all desire distance, which allows them to be an intimidating mystery to their worshippers. As a result, those gods have little influence on the behaviors of their followers when they are out of the range of those gods. In contrast, God has always wanted to be close to His people, and have an influence on their hearts, minds, and lives[101].

The second movement that stands out to me is God's positive regard for everyone. Unlike society, God makes no distinctions between people, but freely loves them all. Isn't this the truth of the simple, yet stirring passage that the apostle John brought out when he penned, *"For God so loved the world that he gave his one and only Son, that whoever believes in him shall not perish but have eternal life"*[102]? Many who grow in bible class learn this passage as a memory verse early on, but the impact of that passage is profound. Note that there are no qualifiers on who can respond to God's promise – it is open to all.

The Jewish nation before Christ missed this truth. Certainly God had chosen them to be His people, and they were His instrument for bringing about the promised Messiah, but the history of the nation of Israel shows just how wrong they were about being God's "only people". The prophet Isaiah proclaimed God's desire for the Jewish nation to be a "light to the Gentiles" – to show non-Jews who God

---

[100] Matthew 28:20
[101] Deuteronomy 6:4-6
[102] John 3:16

really was[103]. The plan was that, by being a light, it would attract people to the true God. God has been working in the lives of all people to bring about a knowledge of Him so that they would find Him[104].

The early Christians also had a hard time wrapping their mind around this fact, at least those with a Jewish background did. Before they became Christians, any non-Jew was a Gentile, unclean, a "dog" in their eyes. Opening up this new kingdom to them was a tough pill to swallow. Look at Peter's struggle in Acts 10 & 11 and you'll get a glimpse of how hard it was to realize that God actually desires a saving relationship with everyone. Peter finally came around and said, *"I now realize how true it is that God does not show favoritism, but accepts men from every nation who fear him and do what is right"*[105]. Peter later in life would go on to write that God is *"not wanting anyone to perish, but everyone to come to repentance"*[106].

But when we look at Peter's life, we see a believer who continued to struggle with this truth. Although God had convinced him that all people were to be invited to be a part of this new kingdom, when an occasion came up in which he felt peer pressure to not be with Gentiles, he caved in. He disassociated himself from Gentile Christians, until Paul called him out face to face about his prejudice[107].

Human nature naturally has us gravitating toward people who are like us – we just feel comfortable around them. As a result, anyone who is different from us can cause

---

[103] Isaiah 42:6; 49:6
[104] Acts 17:24-27
[105] Acts 10:34
[106] 2 Peter 3:9
[107] Galatians 2:11-16

us to feel somewhat uncomfortable. So what do we do? We tend not to hang around those folks. We may not hate them, or even have prejudices toward them, but it is easy to exclude them from our circle of friends or acquaintances just the same. This may convey to those who feel excluded that they are not liked at all.

On a more sinister level, though, prejudice can play a part in our not liking others. Any way that you can divide people up, you can have prejudice – be it gender, race, ethnicity, age, socioeconomic status, etc. And although we tend to think of prejudice in terms of those with more power looking down on those with less power, it cuts both ways. Ever been around those who have little, who stereotype and speak in condescending ways about those who are wealthy? Ever heard minority group individuals use racial slurs against whites? It happens all the time.

When it comes to how the poor are viewed and treated, God has a penchant for those on the underside of society. He made that clear in the instructions given to Moses for the children of Israel that the poor, and those unable to provide for themselves, instead of being despised, should not be oppressed by the wealthy. In fact, one of the issues that God had with the nation of Israel was that poor people were mistreated, rather than helped[108].

With regard to these prejudices, we see in the life of Jesus and in the writings of His followers clear messages about how we should regard others. For instance, even when Jesus came to earth, He chose to come in very humble circumstances. Philip Yancey in his book *"The Jesus I Never Knew"* notes that, "Since God arranged the circumstances in

---

[108] Amos 5:11-12

which to be born on planet earth – without power or wealth, without rights, without justice – his preferential options speak for themselves"[109].

In His teachings, Jesus spoke of care and concern for those in need and said that our eternal destination rests on how we treat others. Look at Matthew 25:31-46 and see by what criterion the "sheep and the goat" will be separated in eternity. Isn't it based upon how we treat *"the least of these"*?

Jesus associated with, ate with, and lived among those who the culture of the day had largely rejected. Rather than ignoring or looking down on a five times over divorcee, for instance, He engaged her in a profound discussion of eternal life and to her revealed that He was the Messiah[110]. This was only one of two times that Jesus directly told someone who He was, and the result was that this woman led many people to believe in Him.

When a leper approached him, Jesus, filled with compassion, reached out and touched the man, healing him not only in body but also in spirit, as Jesus' touch communicated acceptance[111]. Jesus hung out with people that many today might reject and was criticized for that. Jesus' reply was, *"It is not the healthy who need a doctor, but the sick. I have not come to call the righteous, but the sinners"*[112].

Jimmy Dorrell in his book *"Trolls and Truth"* writes that, "Of all the organizations on earth, the church should be

---

[109] Yancey, Philip. (1995). *The Jesus I Never Knew*. Grand Rapids, MI., Zondervan, P. 41.
[110] John 4:4-26
[111] Mark 1:40-42
[112] Mark 2:17

the most inclusive one. Jesus made it so. Going into the highways and byways, He invited the tax collector, the prostitute, the leper, the beggar, the widow, the sick, the criminal, and the formerly demon-possessed into the kingdom of God"[113]. The question for today's church is, "Are these people welcomed today?"

There is a caveat here and a distinction between two groups that we are discussing. One is a group that is underprivileged that may not be accepted by those with more of the world's blessings or goods (such as looks, money, education, talents, etc.). James makes it very clear that discriminating and non-acceptance of others on that sort of basis is wrong[114].

The other group is those who are living lives of sin. Rather than walking in the light, as John puts it[115], they are walking in darkness and sin. Of course, the phrase "hating the sin, but loving the sinner", which is probably based on Jude 22-23, is an accurate way to depict how we need to treat others struggling with sins (although, in reality, we all struggle with sin!). Jesus Himself modeled this. He loved and accepted sinners, but that doesn't mean He was easy on sin. For instance, to a woman caught in the very act of adultery and brought to Jesus for judgment, He told her that He did not condemn her. But His last words to her were, *"Go now and leave your life of sin"*[116].

I am not suggesting that people should be accepted with their sins – that's what the Corinthian church got into

---

[113] Dorrell, Jimmy. (2006). *Trolls and Truth: 14 realities about today's church that we don't want to see.* Birmingham, Alabama, New Hope Publishers, p. 76
[114] James 2:1-7
[115] 1 John 1:7
[116] John 8:11

that caused Paul to rebuke them[117]. But I am suggesting that those who struggle mightily with sins such as alcoholism, homosexuality, addictions, etc. should feel that the church is a place that sees their worth and value as God does, and that serves as an example of the truths of John 3:16.

The bottom line is this: God is a people-person. He loves them and desires to be close to them. Not only has this been true throughout history, but He's also made plans to have people close to Him for eternity. That's why Jesus said, *"In my Father's house are many rooms; if it were not so, I would have told you. I go to prepare a place for you. I am going there to prepare a place for you. And if I go and prepare a place for you, I will come back and take you to be with me that you also may be where I am"*[118].

As followers of His, being with people and working at liking them may be a challenge for some of us. In our personal lives, as well as in our corporate lives as Christians, we need to ask ourselves: Do I like people? Do I accept them? Do I see others through the eyes of Christ as He sees them?

If I could be more like Sadie, I would see the potential in every person I meet and realize the worth and value they have to God. Sadie genuinely enjoys people, smiles at them, and thinks they are worth being around, and I need to work at that as well!

---

[117] I Corinthians 5
[118] John 14:1-3

There is no psychiatrist in the world like a puppy licking your face. –Ben Williams[119]

My goal in life is to be as good of a person my dog already thinks I am. –Author Unknown[120]

---

[119] Retrieved September 5, 2010 from http://www.quotegarden.com/dogs.html
[120] Retrieved September 5, 2010 from http://www.quotegarden.com/dogs.html

...I Would Be More Joyful!

"A happy heart makes the face cheerful" Proverbs 15:13

Don't you just like the stories of Winnie the Pooh and his friends? They are comical, cooperative, and always provide a nice story to live by. One of the characters in particular stands out to me, and that's Eeyore. Do you remember him? He's the blue donkey whose tail is pinned on, and he's always looking at the gloomy side of things. He anticipates the worst all the time, and when things go well, he is sure something will mess them up. Eeyore just has a tough time being joyful and as a result, stays on the negative side of life. He's a nice character, but he misses so much of life because he's focused on what all is going on or will go on. He's the "glass half-empty" type.

When I compare the dispositions of Sadie and Eeyore, there really is no comparison. That dog is flat out joyful! In all the years we've had her, she never turns down a meal! Labs are hearty eaters, and Sadie is no exception! In fact, she eats the same food, twice a day, every day, and she loves it! When it comes time to eat, she is always ready, and she is excited about the whole process.

Labs have a tendency to drool a great deal too. Sadie quickly learned the word "biscuit" and so when I ask her, "Do you want a biscuit?" the fountains of drool begin to flow. I don't usually ask her first, but try to get her one before she's in full-drool mode. Again, she has never turned down a biscuit either!

Sadie also gets two walks a day – one first thing in the morning, and one last thing at night. Being a big dog, she needs the exercise and she enjoys the walks. All we have to say is, "Sadie want to go for a walk?" and she's up, dancing around, ready to be leashed up and head out into the world she hasn't been in for several hours. She enjoys the sights, seeing people, chasing cats, smelling all the smells that are available to her, marking territory, etc. I would have to say that walks are a big deal to Sadie and are the highlights of her day.

If I had to describe her disposition in Winnie the Pooh terms, she is somewhere between Pooh and Tigger. She is a bundle of energy that is always positive, and it is easy to tell that joy is a primary emotion within her.

Life for me, though, isn't always as joyful as I perceive it. Where Sadie is happy with the same food every day, every week, every year, I could be unhappy if I've eaten at the same restaurant twice in a month. Where Sadie enjoys her walks, many times down the same streets twice a day, I might grump about the heat, or the rain, or the snow, etc.

Sadie has a simpler mind than I do (I think!) and so it doesn't take as much for her to be happy. But perhaps that is part of the key – a simpler mind. A mind that focuses on the joyful things in life, instead of looking for the "other shoe to drop".

So what causes people to lose their joy? I think that there are "joy robbers" that creep in and snatch the happiness we should have and leave us feeling miserable as a result. These robbers come in various shapes and forms, and come from different sources, but the end result is always the same: A gloomy or dark outlook on self or the world.

What are some of these job robbers? One prevalent joy robber, *"Discontent"*, lurks about us all the time. One form of this discontent comes through comparing ourselves with others. In psychology the term is the "relative deprivation principle", which in essence states that our happiness is dependent upon how we think we compare with others. We can be happy and thinking that things are just fine, until we run across someone who has better looks, a bigger house, a nicer car, more "toys", etc. The key to cheating this joy robber from stealing our happiness is to make downward comparisons – see how blessed we are in comparison with those less fortunate, and we can find a sense of happiness where we are with what we have.

There is also a pervasive way of thinking that is hard to get away from. The joy robber of "Discontent" here is not in our comparing ourselves to others, but rather in comparing ourselves with ourselves. We are constantly being bombarded with images and messages every day by advertisers who are trying to convince us that what they are selling will bring us the happiness we are looking for. We buy their product, and the short-term high we get from that "thing" quickly evaporates, as we learn that someone else has a better "thing" or that there is now a newer "thing" to be had. If our happiness is dependent upon our looks, athletic abilities, or smarts, they are all short-term values that we will someday lose – it's inevitable.

In the field of Positive Psychology, the emphasis centers on discovering what makes people genuinely happy in their lives. Martin Seligman in his book *"Learned Optimism"*[121] points out a difference between "gratifications" and "pleasures". Pleasures are things that give us joy or happiness that involve the senses, but they don't last long and usually require more and more of the stimulus to feel that sense of happiness. Of course, addictive behaviors fall into

---

[121] Seligman, Martin. (2006). *Learned Optimism: How to change your mind and your life.* New York, NY. Vintage Books.

this category for certain, whether they are addictions to alcohol, drugs, sex, food, etc. All of those things bring a certain degree of pleasure, and if they didn't, we wouldn't do them! Additionally, pleasures can also be things like money and possessions as well.

Research though clearly shows that all of the above do not bring about a lasting happiness – rather they are short-cuts that eventually leave us as unhappy as we were before. Quickly our happiness vanishes as we now think, "I would be happy if I could just have . . ." I like to call it the "when – then" syndrome: *"When I have/am _____, then I'll be happy."*

On the other hand, "gratifications" in the field of Positive Psychology are activities or relationships that bring lasting happiness. In fact, the emotional component that we call "joy" may not even be felt, but rather we have a sense of contentment or satisfaction that comes from engaging in them. Relationships are a big part of this. Those with satisfying marriages and/or good friendships report being happier than those who do not have those relationships. One way then to challenge Discontent is to work on developing closer, more meaningful relationships with our mates, our friends, or our family. We can do this through calling them, sending them letters or cards, praying for them, and talking to them about their lives. Our focus needs to center on others and our relationship with them – not on the short-term pleasures that satisfy only our physical selves.

Also, gratification comes through engaging in challenging activities that use our strengths or talents. Although we may not report being "happy" while doing them as a feeling component, we do feel a sense of purpose while doing them and a sense of satisfaction once they are completed. Rather than just "consuming", as we are when we seek for pleasures, we are "producing", which brings about that sense of purpose.

So another way to avoid being conned by Discontent is to involve ourselves in meaningful work. Work that is gratifying to a person has a creative component to it – it has a purpose beyond just the activity of doing it. Although that work could take a variety of forms, certainly for Christians it takes the form of being active in the kingdom of God. Paul tells the Corinthians that *"your labor in the Lord is not in vain"*[122]. Jesus notes that even a cup of cold water given in His name will not go unrewarded[123]. Anything we do with the purpose of encouraging others to believe in Jesus and encouraging believers to hold onto their faith is work that is meaningful, purposeful, and can bring about joyful living.

Another joy robber is *"Discouragement"* from others. It is so easy to get bummed out and discouraged over a hurtful comment or look, or even worse, apathy from others. We may be trying to live for God, encourage others, and engage in meaningful tasks, only to have someone criticize our ideas, rebuff our friendship, and belittle our work. Talk about a major joy robber! Mark Twain once remarked, "I could live two months on a good compliment"[124]. Many of us are wired that way too. A word of encouragement could really boost our joy and give us energy to move forward, but a word of discouragement can crush us. Solomon wrote, *"The tongue has the power of life and death"*[125], and he was surely right.

---

[122] I Corinthians 15:58
[123] Matthew 10:42
[124] www.brainyquote.com
[125] Proverbs 21:18

Because human beings are wired to be social, we seek the approval and the attention from others. It forms part of our self-worth to be of some value to someone else. Perhaps that's why discouragement cuts so deeply and robs us of our joy – our own self-esteem is threatened.

Since we know that discouraging words are going to come our way if we live with and around others, how can we not allow this joy robber to defeat us? We have to stay around healthy relationships that keep giving us realistic feedback. I'm not talking about setting up an unreal world in which everyone thinks we're wonderful and nothing we do is wrong. That's not real – that's a hot-house environment that won't stand up to the glare of life in the real world. What I am encouraging is developing and maintaining relationships that gently confront us when needed, but also affirm us and our value to them. If we focus only on the negative people about us, it can destroy our joy and rob us of a great deal of contentment, and block our efforts to use our gifts and talents.

"Sin" is another joy robber that each of us contends with on a daily basis. Sins we commit in our lives coupled with the ensuing guilt over things we've done wrong leave us feeling unhappy and should do so. A solution to avoiding this joy robber would be to not sin – and that's a goal to strive for[126]. At the same time, we can't be sinless, and we will still do and think things that are contrary to God's will. We will feel like David who felt as if his sins which had not been confessed were like bones wasting away inside of him[127]. He desperately wanted to be forgiven and asked the Lord to

---

[126] 1 John 2:1
[127] Psalm 32:3

"restore to me the joy of your salvation"[128]. How do we get that joy back? By confessing our sins, knowing that we have Jesus' blood to purify us and we have Jesus himself as an advocate with the Father on our behalf[129]. Being honest about our shortcomings and confessing our sins can restore to us the joy of our salvation.

One other joy robber is "Religious Legalism". Paul addresses a group of believers in Galatians who were previously joyful. Paul asks them, *"What has happened to all your joy?"*[130] They were happy when they learned about Jesus and had become believers. But some had convinced them that they needed more to be happy – more rules, more regulations, more rituals to be pleasing to God. This had made following God to be a burden rather than a pleasure. This is what Jesus referred to when He chided the religious leaders of His day and said of them, *"They tie up heavy loads and put them on men's shoulders, but they themselves are not willing to lift a finger to move them"*[131].

Some leaders in the church make up rules for others to go by. Legalism is an attempt to try to be good enough to be saved by our own efforts. Some do this in an honest attempt to help people stay on the straight and narrow path, while others do it to promote themselves and to have others listen to them. No matter the motive, the results are the same: people are condemned for violating the man-made rules, and the rules are unable to make a person right with God or pure[132]. What they do instead is to turn nice people into mean-spirited ones who are critical of themselves and others,

---

[128] Psalm 51:12
[129] 1 John 1:5-2:2
[130] Galatians 4:15
[131] Matthew 23:4
[132] Colossians 1:20-23

or they turn people away from the church because the rules seem impossible to keep. Others may not even try to follow Christ because they have been convinced that they will never be "good enough" to be saved.

How do we keep this Legalism joy robber from stealing our happiness? We have to separate what people say from what God says. People may make up additional rules for God, but only God's word is binding on us. "Religion" is not a bad word; in fact, James tells us what pure religion is like: caring for those who are downtrodden and disadvantaged in society[133].

Jesus said, *"Come to me, all you who are weary and burdened, and I will give you rest. Take my yoke upon you and learn from me, for I am gentle and humble in heart, and you will find rest for your souls. For my yoke is easy, and my burden is light"*[134]. That doesn't mean the Christian life is easy – nowhere in the Bible is that promised. What it does mean is that following Christ is doable because of what He's already done for us. He's provided a way for us to be right with God that doesn't depend on our own efforts to save ourselves – because we can't do that. We can find rest from trying to be "good enough" to be saved. The burden is light because Jesus is carrying the load! Once you get that, and realize the depths you've been forgiven, then His commands are not burdensome[135].

So we know that Discontent, Discouragement, Sin, and Religious Legalism can be joy robbers that leave us unhappy. How then can we have real joy? As has been suggested above, we can: avoid comparing ourselves with

---

[133] James 1:27
[134] Matthew 11:28-30
[135] 1 John 5:3

others; avoid trying to find happiness in possessions or our physical looks/abilities; develop meaningful relationships that give us honest yet caring and affirming feedback; involve ourselves in activities that engage our strengths and talents; acknowledge sin before God and try to live differently; and keep following the simple truths of God's word rather than arbitrary rules made up by others.

In addition, we live in an amazing world, whose beauty is breathtaking. The moon, stars, mountains, rivers, streams, and oceans provide evidence of God's presence[136]. Every creature has been intricately made and is fascinating. The plants are spectacular in their variety and color. The sky is an amazing canvas with its constantly changing vistas. One way we can have joy is to allow ourselves to see the majesty, might and providence of God all around us.

There are of course things in this life that inevitably will bring us pain or discomfort – that's life. We will have hardships if we follow Christ, we will experience the deaths of loved ones, and we will struggle with our own mortality. Our perspective though of how we deal with these negative events in our lives shapes our happiness or lack thereof. Knowing that we have One who loves us dearly helps us to realize that He is *"the Father of all compassion and the God of all comfort"*[137]. That helps us see hard times as actual occasions in which we can find joy as well[138], because we know that the difficult times are shaping us into the likeness of Christ. In the garden of our lives we can opt to see the roses or the thorns – it's our choice.

---

[136] Psalm 19:1-6
[137] 2 Corinthians 1:3
[138] James 1:2

Of all the people in the world, Christians have the most reason to be joyful! Why? Because we have hope[139]! A short list of those things we have hope in include the fact that we've been forgiven from the past, we have the assurances of God's provision and protection in the present, and the promise of an eternal life with God where there is no death, no crying, and no tears. How good is that? Joy is also one of the fruits of the Spirit that we should be showing in our lives[140]. A "joyless Christian" is an oxymoron!

If I could be more like Sadie, I would be less like Eeyore and instead focus my attention on the good things in my life, and have more joy as a result. Finding pleasure in simple things that God has blessed me with would certainly make life more enjoyable as well!

---

[139] Romans 12:12
[140] Galatians 5:22-23

...I Would Listen to My Master's Voice!

> *"The ox knows his master, the donkey his owner's manger, but Israel does not know, my people do not understand."*
> *Isaiah 1:3*

Nipper the dog is one of the most famous dogs in the world. He was born in 1884 in Bristol, England, and in 1898 an artist painted a portrait of Nipper sitting in front of the bell of a gramophone. He later entitled his picture as "His Master's Voice", and that picture and slogan has been a part of the music industry for over 100 years now. In fact, the HMV Group ("His Master's Voice") is one of the leaders in the music, gaming, and video business today. The sight of Nipper cocking his head at the sound coming from the bell of the gramophone is a well-known icon, and a 4-ton statue of Nipper sits on top of a building on Broadway in Albany, New York.

Although Sadie was born over 100 years after Nipper, she too listens for her master's voice. We can have a roomful of people over and there can be conversation going on all around, but when I speak, she perks up her ears and looks at me, even if I am not speaking to her. Debra jokes that it is like the old investment company advertising that said, "When E.F. Hutton speaks, people listen." When I speak, Sadie listens. She can pick my voice out of the crowd, and if I am in another part of the house and she hears me talking, here she comes. She thinks that if I am talking, whatever it is about or to whomever it is, she should be listening. It is really comical at times how in tune with my voice she is.

What about my Master's voice? Well, sad to say, sometimes it is a different story. There are *so* many voices that compete for my attention. Things that seem to demand urgent attention, things that are diversions from more important tasks that need to be done, as well as temptations, all compete with the Master's voice. It reminds me of the Sirens in Greek mythology – the legendary sisters whose music and singing was so beautiful that it lured unsuspecting sailors passing by to jump overboard to try to swim to the island to see them. Boats were shipwrecked, and many a sailor's bones were strewn about the island, having died as a result of trying to follow the sounds of their voices.

Now, of course, that's mythology, but it does reflect the realities around us in life. So many things have an alluring appeal to them and tempt us to shift our attention from the One's voice we should be most attuned to. Jesus said, *"The man who enters by the gate is the shepherd of his sheep. The watchman opens the gate for him, and the sheep listen to his voice. He calls his own sheep by name and leads them out. When he has brought out all his own, he goes on ahead of them, and his sheep follow him because they know his voice. But they will never follow a stranger; in fact, they will run away from him because they do not recognize a stranger's voice"*[141].

I see two problems that I as a "sheep" am confronted with in Jesus' analogy. One problem is: how well do I recognize His voice? If I don't spend time in His word, how will I recognize His voice in my life? David wrote, *"I have hidden your word in my heart that I might not sin against you"*[142] as a way of knowing God and thus avoiding sin. How can I recognize what is right and what is wrong unless I am familiar with the voice of the Master? Sin may come cleverly disguised, but if I know my Master, it should be clearer to me

---

[141] John 10:2-5
[142] Psalm 119:11

what the good path I should be on is like, and which evil path I need to not step foot on.

This is the same challenge that Moses gave the tribes of Israel when he told them, *"This day I call heaven and earth as witnesses against you that I have set before you life and death; blessings and curses. Now choose life, so that you and your children may live and that you may love the Lord your God, listen to his voice, and hold fast to him. For the Lord is your life…"*[143] Moses knew that the people would encounter other voices in their wanderings and their conquest of the Promised Land, ones that would lead them to destruction if they followed those voices.

So I need to become more and more familiar with the voice of my Master if I am to hear Him guide me in my life. By tuning into His voice, it will help me to drown out those other sounds that compete for attention. How can I best do this? Well, according to the Greek myths, there were only two ships that survived passing the island of the Sirens without loss of life. Three different methods were used to avoid being lured into death by the voices.

The first method was used on the ship that Odysseus captained. He had his men put wax in their ears so that they could not hear the music and be tempted by it. Although in the myth this worked for them, in reality it is not a complete solution to the problem. They didn't hear the Sirens, but they also couldn't hear anything else. This reminds me of the man who has an evil spirit leave him, and when the evil spirit comes back, the "house" is unoccupied, and so he takes up residence in the man with seven other spirits more wicked than itself[144]. There was an absence of evil, but there was

---

[143] Deuteronomy 30:19-20
[144] Matthew 12:43-45

also an absence of good. Edmund Burke once said, "All that is necessary for the triumph of evil is that good men do nothing"[145], and Ayn Rand added that "The spread of evil is a symptom of a vacuum"[146]. Blocking out evil is a great idea, but if that is the only course of action, then at some point evil will creep back in and other voices will be heard.

The second method that was used to avoid being destroyed by the lure of the Sirens' music Odysseus used himself. He wanted to hear them, but to keep from jumping overboard he had his men lash him to the mast of the ship. As they sailed past the island, he was tortured in his mind because the temptations were so strong, yet he was forcibly prevented from following them. He survived this ordeal, but what a terrible way to deal with the voices. Would this work for me? I think that it would lead to being double-minded – having a foot in one world and one foot in another.

Regarding the voice of money that calls to us to trust in it, Jesus said, *"No one can serve two masters. Either he will hate the one and love the other, or he will be devoted to the one and despise the other. You cannot serve both God and money"*[147]. What is true for that voice is true for other things or relationships that would compete with our Master for our allegiance. There are some times when drastic measures need to be taken in order to deal with the other voices of sin in our lives[148], but God also wants us to have a pure mind, a single focus on Him[149], rather than putting

---

[145] www.quotationspage.com
[146] www.quotationspage.com
[147] Matthew 6:24
[148] Matthew 5:27-30
[149] James 4:8

ourselves in temptation's path to try to listen to those voices as well.

The third method in the Greek mythology was the one used by the second ship. Jason and his Argonauts also had to sail by the island that had the Sirens on them. They were saved though because Orpheus, one of the Argonauts, played more beautiful music which captured the attention of the crew and diverted their attention from listening to the Sirens. To me, this method makes the most sense. Rather than just blocking out the music only, or torturing oneself by listening to the Sirens' music and trying not to follow it, these sailors listened to another voice – one that was more pure and beautiful.

What about me? I believe that by my listening to the beautiful words of my Master, it can divert my attention from other voices as well. Like Jason's Argonauts, I can pay attention to the sound of His voice that is clearer, purer, and more beautiful as well. That can only happen if I listen, though.

A second problem that I see with Jesus' analogy of the sheep and shepherd comes about when discussing the "stranger". Notice again what Jesus says about the stranger's voice: the sheep don't follow him because they don't know him. Turning that around, if I follow a stranger's voice – is it because I *do* know him? Perhaps one of the problems I have in wanting to follow a stranger's voice is that I have spent too much time with "strangers". Rather than being unfamiliar, their voices are ones that I have heard and I have followed before – with disastrous results. Yet, the allure and promise of their voices is that the next time I follow them it will be different. They will deliver on their promises and I will be happier as a result.

So how do I go about "de-strangering" (if I can make up that word!) my life? First, I know that I need to see the strangers clearly for who they are: imposter voices that only seek to harm me. Like bait on a hook, the attraction is there, but it is a false veneer that hides real pain and suffering. Second, I need to do what most mothers tell their children to do: Don't talk to strangers! I need to avoid those voices that call me, who make their promises appealing, and who try to captivate my attention. There can't be any compromise with sin, compromise with procrastination, or compromise with situations that lead me away from my Master's voice. Putting wax in my ears (not doing evil) is not enough. Lashing myself to a mast (flirting with temptation) is dangerous and leads to torture. My focus has to be on listening to The Voice which has my best interest in mind, which seeks to lead me to those green pastures and still waters where I am really taken care of. My Master's voice is the only voice I need to be in tune with.

To focus on the Master's voice, I need to be selective in my hearing as well. I need to be dead to the other voices that clamor for my attention. Like the words of the old hymn, *"A New Creature"*, I need to be dead to the other voices that call me. The first verse and chorus of the song says:

Buried with Christ, my blessed Redeemer,

Dead to the old life of folly and sin;

Satan may call me, the world may entreat me,

There is no voice that answers within.

Dead to the world, to voices that call me,

Living anew, obedient but free,

Dead to the joys that once did enthrall me,
Yet 'tis not I, Christ liveth in me.[150]

    Sadie clearly heard my voice, her Master's voice, and paid special attention when I spoke. If I could be more like Sadie, I too would quit listening to strangers and the music they try to play for me. I would pay more special attention to my Master's voice, and thus not only avoid the shipwrecks in my life, but also enjoy the guidance, protection, and care that following His voice will bring me.

    I may not be the only one who struggles with other voices too. *Whose* voice are *you* listening to?

Dogs have given us their absolute all. We are the center of their universe. We are the focus of their love and faith and trust. They serve us in return for scraps. It is without a doubt the best deal man has ever made. –Roger Caras[151]

---

[150] T.O. Chisholm. (1935). *A New Creature.* In *Songs of Faith and Praise.* West Monroe, LA., Howard Publishing Co., Inc., 1994, p. 619.
[151] Retrieved September 5, 2010 from http:www.quotegarden.com/dogs.html

...I Would Be More Persistent in Prayer!

"So I say to you: Ask and it will be given you; seek and you will find; knock and the door will be opened to you." Luke 11:9

Sadie is very persistent about a couple of things in her life. One is suppertime. When it comes time for her to eat, about 4:00pm every day, she has already been ready and often been asking for 2 hours. What she will do is this: She will sashay up next to the couch, and then lie down right by Debra's feet. It's hard not to notice a 70 lb. dog lying on your feet. Her requests for supper involve two main tactics: One is staring. She can fix her eyes on Debra and not break her eye contact. When she is told "No, it's not time," she just glances away for a few minutes, either licking her paws or laying her head down briefly, and then raises her head and resumes the stare. She is really good at it!

Her other tactic is to paw swat. She takes one paw and swats it on Debra's foot. If she is lying across the room, she'll do the same thing: take one big ole paw, and swat it on the ground while looking at you. And she doesn't stop there. If you don't respond in a timely fashion, in her opinion, she'll paw swat again. Like staring, she is stubborn and can keep this up for a long, long time. Of course, she is in a not-so-subtle way trying to communicate her belief that it is time to eat! Although she has not gotten Debra to budge on the feeding schedule, with Sadie, hope springs eternal that one day Debra will break!

Another thing Sadie is persistent about is her walks. She lives for them! When she thinks it is time to go, she'll go into the laundry room where her leash is and stare at it, and then come back and stare at you. It's almost as if she has a clock in her head, a time-table that her world is supposed to run on, and she does her best to get the humans in her world on board with her schedule. Like with her eating, Sadie is pretty insistent that her two walks a day occur, despite what the weather is outside. Being a Lab, the colder and wetter it is, the better she likes it!

Somewhere Sadie has acquired (or perhaps she always had it!) the ability to be persistent in her requests. She doesn't bark, she doesn't pitch a fit, she just doggedly (no pun intended) sticks to her intentions of getting our attention and convincing us to go along with her ideas.

As I have thought about her persistence, I am struck by my own lack of persistence in asking my Master for things. Sadie stays with it until she gets what she's wanting, but I often pray once or twice and move on to other things. Perhaps my sporadic efforts with prayer, as well as the lack of persistence I see in others, come from errors in the way we view and use prayer.

James writes that, *"You do not have, because you do not ask God"*[152]. Why? Perhaps it could be a lack of faith overall in prayer. We think, "Will it work?" and ask doubtfully. I think a funny story in the book of Acts occurs when believers are praying for the release of Peter from jail[153]. God sends an angel and miraculously delivers him, but when he shows up at the door where the Christians are praying, they don't believe he has really been freed. The attitude is, "Don't interrupt us, we're praying for Peter's release" and he's standing at the door! Coupled with that may also be an attitude that says, "If our prayers are not answered, then is God's credibility in question?" We may fear that an

---

[152] James 4:2
[153] Acts 12:1-17

unanswered prayer may poke a hole in our faith about God's providence and provision in our lives.

Our lack of asking could be due to a busy schedule. Many of us are harried, hurried, and scrambling to keep up most of the time. To add to our schedule an extended time for prayer is overwhelming. The Psalmist wrote down God's counsel to people and penned, *"Be still, and know that I am God"*[154]. This is similar to the words Moses spoke to the slaves who were leaving Egypt but who were panicked at the approach of the armies of Pharaoh. Moses told them, *"The Lord will fight for you; you need only to be still"*[155]. Sometimes we don't ask because we have too much going on when we need to be still, talk to God, and allow peace to be a product of that encounter.

Some may not be persistent in prayer because they are afraid of a "no" answer. God may not grant our prayer request as we would like for Him to, and the result may be a damaged faith. We are tempted to forget that He told Moses "No" about going into the Promised Land, He told Paul "No" when asked about his thorn in the flesh being removed, and He told His own Son "No" when Jesus asked in the garden that the cup of suffering be removed. Of course, an answer of "No" is not what we want to hear or see, and it does take great faith to continue to hold onto God's promises when the heavens seem as brass – and our prayers seem to be bouncing back at us with a resounding "No."

Believers may be tempted to not pray about a situation because it may mean that God will have them take a path that they don't want to go on. Hannah Hurnard relates such a situation that the main character, Much Afraid,

---

[154] Psalm 46:10
[155] Exodus 14:14

encounters in her delightful book, *"Hind's Feet on High Places"*[156]. She is asked why she doesn't call on the Great Shepherd to help her get to the High Places, and she says that she is afraid that he will want her to go up a narrow path to get there, and she is afraid of going on that path! She doesn't want to ask because it will mean facing her own fears. Similarly, praying to God about things in our lives may signal a commitment we are not ready to make. There could be some challenges we do not really want to take or some temptation we really don't want to give up just yet.

Another barrier to persistence in prayer may be pride – we see asking as a sign of weakness. We think, "The Lord helps those who help themselves" (which is not in the Bible, by the way!), and we try to gut things out on our own. We proceed with our own strength, our own wisdom, and our own resources. We then wonder why, as we pick ourselves up from the messes we're in, things didn't work out! We didn't resist some temptation, we didn't accomplish some task, and we misjudged situations badly – all because we didn't ask for help. The rugged individualism that is a cultural trait of America doesn't make for a good Christian life – one that is to be dependent upon God for help.

At the opposite end of the spectrum from pride is low self-esteem, and those struggling with that may believe that praying for themselves is selfish and self-centered. We're tempted to think, "My life is not that important, and God has many more problems to deal with than my puny requests" and then we don't ask. What we miss is our value to God, and how much he earnestly wants to fill our requests. Remember Jesus' teaching on prayer? He told His disciples

---

[156] Hurnard, Hannah. (2005). *Hind's Feet on High Places.* Shippensburg, PA, Destiny Image Publishers.

that if a good father would give good gifts to his own children who ask him, how much more would our Father in heaven give good gifts to those who ask Him[157]? Jesus prayed for Himself, Paul prayed for himself, and we are encouraged to bring our requests to God about all things[158].

Another barrier to persistent prayer is the presence of sin in our lives. We may have sin that we have not confessed, have not repented of, which stands between ourselves and God. Adam and Eve, after enjoying a close relationship with God, actually hid after they had disobeyed Him because of their shame. Shame can also keep us from approaching God because we know that there is a problem that needs to be addressed. Of course, that barrier can be easily removed with a humble heart and an honest request if we will just ask. The publican's prayer has to be one of the shortest prayers in the Bible, *"God, have mercy on me, a sinner,"* but Jesus said that the publican went home justified as a result[159]. God has always been eager to forgive His people who earnestly seek it – that's the meaning of the story Jesus told about the lost son and his father who waits for him to come home[160].

One other reason we may not be as persistent in prayer is that we have low expectations. Jesus in His teachings encourages followers to ask, seek, and knock, and to not give up! Rather than having low expectations, He challenges us to have high ones instead. He gave two examples to prod us into asking in a persistent manner. The first was when he told about a man who has unexpected guests and needed some food from a friend to help feed them. Jesus said the friend will eventually help out, not because the

---

[157] Matthew 7:9-11
[158] Philippians 4:6
[159] Luke 18:9-14
[160] Luke 15:11-24

persistent man is a buddy, but rather, *"because of the man's boldness he will get up and give him as much as he needs"*[161].

The second example Jesus later told his disciples was about a widow in an unfair situation[162]. She needs justice, but the unjust judge is reluctant to hear her. Finally he relents, due to her constancy of asking, and Jesus says that if a crooked judge will grant a request, how much more will a loving God do!

Prayer is, of course, not just talking with our Father; it should also, like the widow, be the willingness to ask imploringly for what we need. Becky Blackmon in her book, *The Begging Place*, says it best when she writes, "It is one thing to pray, but it is an entirely different thing to beg, plead, implore. At the Begging Place hearts are poured out to God, often with many tears. It is a place of deepest entreaty we can possibly offer up to Him. At the Begging Place our prayers are places of the deepest nature, as our lives are upset with conflict, problems, sin, and Satan's attacks. We have a reason to be there"[163].

In all of the obstacles to our being persistent in prayer, there is a common element missing: faith. At the end of the parable about the widow above, Jesus concludes it by asking, *"However, when the Son of Man comes will he find faith on the earth"*[164]? A lack of faith is a common downfall – not believing prayer will work, not having the faith to slow down and believe that God will help us calm our busy

---

[161] Luke 11:8
[162] Luke 18:1-8
[163] Blackmon, Becky. (2006). *The Begging Place.* Huntsville, AL., Publishing Designs, Inc., p. 23.
[164] Luke 18:8

worlds, not having the faith to weather a potential "No" response, not believing we need God's help or not believing we are important enough to bother Him, not believing He will help us accomplish a difficult task in our lives or conquer a particular area of temptation.

In his letter to the church at Rome, Paul penned that *"faith comes from hearing the message, and the message is heard through the word of Christ"*[165]. For believers today, reading and reflecting on God's word increases our faith as we see His fidelity to His people throughout time. We see Him working in the lives of others, and we have no reason to doubt that the same God who was operating in the lives of His followers then is not operating in our lives today. The writer of Hebrews also adds that *"faith is being sure of what we hope for and certain of what we do not see"*[166]. When we can develop that kind of faith, it allows us to approach God's throne with confidence[167]. That's what Paul encouraged followers of Christ to do when he told the church at Colossae to *"devote yourselves to prayer"*[168] and the believers at Thessalonica *"pray continually"*[169]. The followers of Christ did not doubt God and His faithfulness, but rather believed that He would listen to them and take action on their petitions.

When I reflect on Sadie's persistence, I see that she has no reason to doubt me either. Food is always provided, and she knows that sooner or later she will be fed. She also knows that a walk will be coming, and so she stays persistent in her efforts to make happen what she is certain will happen

---

[165] Romans 10:17
[166] Hebrews 11:1
[167] Hebrews 4:16
[168] Colossians 4:2
[169] 1 Thessalonians 5:17

– a walk! So, if I, an imperfect master of a dog, can instill in her that kind of faith, what kind of faith should I have with my Master who is completely faithful to His promises?

If I could be more like Sadie, I would work at deepening my faith and praying with persistence. I would believe more fully that I have God's ear – not because of myself, but because of what He's promised. I would be paw-swatting and staring at God more consistently, and find a God who listens and answers me because He loves me. What a blessing!

I talk to him when I'm lonesome like; and I'm sure he understands. When he looks at me so attentively, and gently licks my hand; then he rubs his nose on my tailored clothes, but I never say naught thereat. For the good Lord knows I can buy more clothes, but never a friend like that. –W. Dayton Wedgefarth[170]

---

[170] Retrieved September 5, 2010 from http:www.quotegarden.com/dogs.html

...I Would Long for My Master's Return!

"I have fought the good fight, I have finished the race, I have kept the faith. Now there is in store for me the crown of righteousness, which the Lord, the righteous Judge, will award to me on that day – and not only to me, but also to all who have longed for his appearing." 2 Timothy 4:7-8

    Something funny happened one morning when I went out for a morning jog. You see, I like to get up early in the morning and run, and when I come back, I hook Sadie up to the leash and we go for a walk. She loves it, and it gives me a cool down from my run.

    It was a summer morning, and the sun comes up early, so I had opened the blinds and then taken off on my run. When I got back, Debra was wide awake. "Did you know what Sadie did when you left?" she asked. "No, I don't have the slightest idea," I replied. "Well, she saw you running down the street without her, and she began howling like a wounded coyote." Sadie had never howled before, and being a big dog, she could really let out a good howl! It seems that she was hurt that I was leaving without her, and she wanted to go too! She began, after that morning, a habit of howling whenever she catches me leaving her to go out for a run. I have to make sure she either doesn't see me leave or that the blinds are shut so she can't witness my departure. I think it is really funny, but bless her heart, Debra, who has to listen to it, is not amused!

    Sadie also does two other things when I leave the house for any reason. She goes to a window where she can look down the street, and she lies down, places her big head on the window sill, and waits for me to return. We find the drool-marks on the window sills where she lays her head.

She doesn't move but just stays there, focusing her eyes on the horizon to see me coming back home. When she sees me, she gets up, and begins her whole body wag as she barks anxiously for me to come through the door. Also, when I leave to go hunting early on winter mornings, she wakes up and stays up until I return. She won't go back to bed because she is anticipating my return. Again, poor Debra is the recipient of Sadie's antics, and rather than being able to sleep in when I slip out at 4:00am, she usually has to get up too and stay up because Sadie is up.

Sadie really waits for my return and is so glad when I come back. Occasionally I try to sneak in without her knowing and I have found her sleeping, especially after she has gotten older, but it is still very rare that I am able to return without her knowing it. She believes I am coming back and she is waiting.

When I think about my Master's return, I must confess that more often than not I am not waiting. It's not that I don't believe The Lord is going to return; it's just that it is so easy to get caught up in other things that divert my attention from His return. I believe that there is also a difference between my death, which would usher me into the presence of my Lord, and His coming, which would do the same thing. In a way, the result is the same, but at the same time, wanting His return signifies that I am ready for that encounter, whereas wanting to wait until I die actually means I want to put off meeting the Lord just yet.

There are several reasons it is easy to get caught up in the here and now and not be looking forward as much as I should be. Part of it is unfinished business. There are certain things that I want to finish up here, although His coming would render them null and void. There is a desire to finish projects, put things in order, prepare things for those who will be left behind, etc. But again, if the Lord comes, then those things are really irrelevant.

Another part of not being ready yet is that there are people who I would like to see get their lives right with God, and if my Master returned today, they would not be in a saved relationship with Him. Knowing that should prompt me to have more urgency to talk with them, encourage them, pray for them, while it is today, rather than putting off those discussions and actions until later.

Part of it may be due to materialism. I have a wife who is a terrific companion, a comfortable house, two cars that run, a job that pays my bills, clothes to wear, too much food to eat, and my needs are more than supplied. (And of course, I have Sadie too!) In that type of environmental cocoon, it's easy to have one's mind shift from the eternal to the worldly. It's not that I don't want to go to heaven – I just focus more on my going to heaven at the end of my life rather than on anticipating His coming before that time. Do you get the difference? I am ready to go to Him when I am through here – but that's on my terms when I am ready. I should instead want Him to come sooner than that. Part of that again could be the relatively pleasant life I am blessed to live. In addition, Jesus' warnings about not putting anything before Him, relationships or possessions, pulls at me and causes me to re-evaluate what I want more – my Lord, or my life now?

I know I'm not the only one who has been tempted to shift his focus from God to this earth. The Jewish people returning from captivity faced the same temptation. The prophet Haggai voiced God's words to the former exiles to think about God and build His house. They were so focused on building their own dwellings that they had largely forgotten about God's temple, and so God asks, *"Is it a time for you yourselves to be living in your paneled houses, while this house remains a ruin"*[171]? The Jewish leaders in Jesus' time also were so focused on keeping their positions of power and stability that they missed the Messiah who was right in their midst, the one they were praying about and waiting for[172].

Part of my lack of focus on His coming may be also due to the fact that He hasn't come yet. I can hear someone say, "A day with the Lord is as a thousand years" and I know that, but in my short lifetime, He hasn't come. Not only that, it's been nearly 2,000 years since He's been gone.

Why? What is He waiting for? Now seems to be as good a time as any. In fact, as I look back on history since His departure, there have been some times that I would have thought for sure He would have come. Just in the past century, a good time to come would have been during the Great Depression, during World War II to stop Nazi atrocities, during other genocides in Soviet Russia, Rwanda and Sudan, or before the World Trade Center Buildings were destroyed by crazed religious fanatics. Any of those times and countless more would have stopped so much heartache and bloodshed and misery in the lives of millions.

When I ask that question, "Why not now?" I am forced to think about how the nation of Israel must have asked that very same question. During times of oppression by either neighboring nations or world powers, they must have cried out for the Lord. We see in the prophets some of those questions asked, such as that by Habakkuk when he prayed,

---

[171] Haggai 1:4
[172] John 11:45-50

"How long, O Lord, must I call for help, but you do not listen? Or cry out to you, 'Violence!' but you do not save? Why do you tolerate wrong? Destruction and violence are before me; there is strife, and conflict abounds"[173]. An anguished cry from one seeking the intervention of the Lord – a sign of His justice, His coming, which would end the injustices he saw on a daily basis.

The only answer I can come up with is that God has His own timetable for when He will send Jesus again. Jesus doesn't even know when the Father plans on calling an end to this world and bringing to a conclusion life on this planet[174]. God, who was before time and transcends time, does things when He knows they are best to happen. Abraham waited 25 years to have his promised child, the children of Israel were enslaved 400 years before they could leave Egypt, Joshua and Caleb had to wait 40 years because of the faithlessness of others to enter the land promised to them, exiled Israel had to wait 70 years before being brought back from captivity. God's people have always been a waiting people, which foster a faith in Him and dependence upon Him instead of ourselves.

Jesus even used several parables to urge His followers to keep watch and to be prepared for His return. During His last week, when His time of betrayal and crucifixion was within 48 hours, He told His disciples to be ready for when His second coming would happen. He told them a story about virgins who were prepared for the wedding banquet and were admitted, and others who were not prepared who did not get

---

[173] Habakkuk 1:2-3
[174] Matthew 24:36

to participate. He ended that by saying, *"Therefore keep watch, because you do not know the day or the hour"*[175].

Jesus also told them a story about a wealthy man who needed to be gone on a trip, but in his absence entrusted three servants to take care of a portion of his property. Two of the servants worked and were faithful, but the third one neglected to do what he should have done. As a result, when the master came back, that servant was cast out into darkness[176].

Paul praises believers in Thessalonica because they were waiting for Jesus to come from heaven[177]. He ends his letter to them encouraging all believers to be alert and ready for the coming of the Lord – to anticipate it so that we aren't caught off guard and unaware[178]. Peter echoes the same concern as he urges Christians to live holy and godly lives, looking forward to the day of God[179]. As Paul closes out his first letter to the followers in Corinth, he wrote, *"Come, O Lord"*[180], and John closes out the revelation given to him by Jesus by uttering the last prayer of the church, *"Amen. Come, Lord Jesus"*[181].

So that brings it back to you and me. Do we have that same desire, that same anticipation, that same longing for our Master to return? With His return on my mind, I need to keep my priorities in better order, talk now with people I need to talk with, and do things today rather than putting them off until a later time. If I could be more like Sadie, I would also

---

[175] Matthew 25:13
[176] Matthew 25:14-30
[177] 1 Thessalonians 1:9-10
[178] 1 Thessalonians 5:1-11
[179] 2 Peter 3:8-14
[180] 1 Corinthians 16:22
[181] Revelation 22:10

keep my eyes clear from the things in this life that can cloud my vision and focus more intently on the horizon, waiting for my Master to come back again.

The Master's Timing...

"There is a time for everything, and a season for every activity under heaven: a time to be born and a time to die..."
Ecclesiastes 3:1-2

The day was July 10. For several months, our old friend had been struggling with her health. She had hip dysplasia for years, which we had treated successfully with food and medication, but now it was getting to where that was not working for her anymore. Getting up was a real struggle, and she also struggled at times to just walk.

Being an inside dog, she had been housetrained within 7 days as a pup, so we never had a problem with her going to the bathroom in the house. Now, at over thirteen years old, she was occasionally losing bowel control. She would try to get to the back door to go out, but sometimes she was just unable to make it before defecating. She would have an "I'm sorry" look in her eyes because that is not what she wanted to do. She was embarrassed at having made the mess – that's not how she was used to living her life. We would just clean it up, love on her, and reassure her that it was all right and we understood.

Well, we had taken Sadie to the vet about 2 weeks before to get a shot that would relieve her of some of the pain she was experiencing. It worked a little and she was able to move a little bit better, but the medication was not able to control her pain as much as we would have liked for it to.

That day, July 10, Sadie struggled to her feet to go out. She made it, but she could hardly move once outside. She stood stiffly, as if every movement was just too painful to make. I knew then what we needed to do. We could prevent this, and she did not need to deal with this pain when we could end it. Sadie had lived with dignity and needed to be allowed to die with dignity as well.

I talked with Debra and said, "It's time," tears welling up in my eyes. I called the vet's office and, with a shaky voice, told the receptionist what it was I needed to make an appointment for. She was gracious and told me we could bring her on in.

As I helped Sadie into the car, Debra and I knew that this was the last trip, the last time to pet her, talk with her, love on her – and the emotions were overwhelming. We made the short journey to the vet's office, and I took her on into the examination room. I had taken a blanket with me, and I had Sadie lay down on it. It was tough for her to lay down, but she made it, and rested comfortably while we waited for our vet, Dr. Gregory. When he came in the room, I could hardly speak. Sadie's big tail though was thumping as she saw him, as it did with everybody she met. With a huge lump in my throat, I told him what we had seen that morning with Sadie and that I thought it was time – time for her to be put to sleep. He nodded his head in agreement. We had talked with him numerous times before about the Labs that he had, and he had told us about having to put them down, so he knew the signs well. He agreed with me that the most humane thing to do was to let her pass away rather than prolonging her suffering.

The process was relatively painless for Sadie. One shot to cause her to be sedated, and another shot to slow and stop her heart and respiration. As Dr. Gregory gave the first shot, everything inside of me was screaming, *"No! How can I do this to my best friend? I'm not ready! She's been my best friend for over 13 years – and I can't let her go, not now!"*

Sadie though was calm and trusted me that whatever she was experiencing, it was for her own good.

He left the room and waited for a few moments to allow the first shot to work. I loved on Sadie, stroking her black coat, petting her head, talking to her reassuringly, and she remained so calm. Then the door opened and Dr. Gregory returned with the second injection. I dreaded his return because I knew that there was absolutely no way we could go back.

Again, part of me agonized with thoughts of, *"Please, no!"* but at the same time, it *was* time. As he gave her the second injection, her breathing slowed down and she calmly drifted off as I held her. It was as peaceful a passing as I have ever witnessed, but for me it was the toughest loss I have ever encountered. He left us and allowed me time to be with her before leaving. I again spoke to her, loved on her, and cried as I buried my head in her black coat of fur one last time.

Well, that day was filled with deep grief and anguish. For days later, just the very thought of her or the mention of her name would bring a flood of tears. Her bed, her food dish, her toys, her blanket – all painful reminders of the friend who would no longer be with us.

Loss with all of its associated emotions is a difficult task in life to endure. In my years of counseling others who have suffered losses, I have found that some lose hope, grow bitter, while others deepen their faith and resolve their relationship with the Master. Part of losing a loved one involves the stark reality that this world is not permanent and it's not our home. As Peter reminded the followers of Christ, we are really strangers and foreigners in this world[182].

Cancer survivor and grief counselor Randy Becton understood this when he penned this prayer of one in grief,

"Lord, I better understand that this world

Is filled with sorrow.

Thank you for

Saving this world.

We love and lose.

You, not this world,

Are our home.

I praise you for teaching me

Through my sorrow to trust you."[183]

Sadie left this life in her master's arms, in her master's care, and in her master's timing. She didn't fuss or complain, and although she didn't really comprehend that she was dying, she trusted her master that whatever it was she was going through, it was all right.

David understood death and dying, and the implicit trust of the sheep in its shepherd when he wrote, *"Even*

---

[182] 1 Peter 2:11
[183] Becton, Randy. (1993). *Everyday comfort: Readings for the first month of grief.* Grand Rapids, MI., Baker Book House Company, P. 89.

though I walk through the valley of the shadow of death, I will fear no evil, for you are with me... "[184] David trusted that his Shepherd would be with him, even through the dark veil of death. If I could have the faith of Sadie, I would trust that no matter what happens in my life, that it is in my Master's timing and care. I may not be aware of my own ending – how or when it comes – but I know that I too will be wrapped in my Master's arms as he loves me through the valley of the shadow of death.

> *"Near this spot are deposited the remains of one who possessed beauty without vanity, strength without insolence, courage without ferocity, and all the virtues of man, without his vices." –Lord Byron*

---

[184] Psalm 23:4

Made in the USA
Lexington, KY
03 March 2018